PRIVACY FOR SOFTWARE ENGINEERS: A PRACTICAL GUIDE TO DATA PROTECTION AND COMPLIANCE

Concepts, Techniques and Best Practices for Implementing Privacy in Software Development

Marison Souza

CONTENTS

INTRODUCTION

Privacy isn't just about following rules – it's about gaining people's trust. If a company loses this trust, no amount of compliance will save it. Today, every click, purchase or registration leaves digital traces. And if you're a software engineer, part of your job is to ensure that this data is treated with respect before an issue makes headlines. More than meeting legal obligations, the trust of those who choose to interact with these companies is at stake.

And trust, as we know, is built over time, but can be destroyed in one click.

Those leading this change are the teams dedicated to privacy. Roles such as Data Protection Officer (DPO) emerge as strategic figures, connecting legal requirements to practical operation, acting both as guardians of compliance and defenders of privacy rights. Alongside them, Chief Privacy Officers, analysts and privacy engineers form essential teams to address the growing challenges of protecting data while driving business efficiency and innovation.

What intrigues me about this scenario is the abyss that persists between discourse and practice. Despite regulations and well-defined objectives, technical professionals are often faced with the same question:

How to implement this in practice?

This gap between theoretical knowledge and technical execution was what motivated me to explore and share this topic.

Digital channels exemplify this complexity well. They are the front line where data flows in immense volumes, at a speed that is impossible to predict and with a constant risk of leakage or misuse of personal data. Every click, form or transaction generates a flow of information that needs to be monitored, protected and handled responsibly. In this environment, any failure can have devastating consequences, both for users and organizations.

Protecting data goes beyond technical skill — it's about respect. Here, you'll see how to put that into practice.

Privacy is not a luxury, but a fundamental right that must guide every decision made by creators, developers and operators of technological systems. This reinforces the need for a new generation of professionals: people who not only master the fundamentals of information security, but who also know how to transform privacy principles into technical reality.

Software engineers, developers and systems architects occupy a central position in this change. They are no longer just tool builders; They are guardians of privacy, responsible for incorporating data protection practices directly into code, configurations, systems and operational processes. These professionals collaborate with security experts, legal teams, and, above all, users themselves, to create solutions that are both functional and ethical.

The most inspiring aspect of this scenario is the potential for innovation that privacy brings. Contrary to what many imagine, implementing data protection practices does not restrict creativity, but challenges it.

How to design systems that respect privacy without compromising efficiency?

How to offer transparency and control to the user without compromising the experience?

These questions raise the bar for solutions and drive a new level of excellence.

If there's one thing I've learned, it's that privacy and data protection cannot be achieved in isolation. They require collaboration. It is necessary for technicians to talk to the legal team, for operational teams to listen to users and for everyone, together, to recognize privacy as more than an obligation: an opportunity to shape a fairer and safer digital future.

Information Security (IS) and privacy share a symbiotic relationship, but unequal in their dependence: while IS can exist without privacy, protecting systems, networks and data from external and internal threats, privacy cannot survive without the foundations of IS. Without robust confidentiality, integrity and availability controls, personal data becomes vulnerable to unauthorized access, leaks and manipulations, compromising people's fundamental rights. SI is the foundation that supports privacy, providing the tools and practices necessary to ensure that personal data is protected, while privacy adds an ethical and regulatory layer, guiding how this information should be treated. This parallel highlights that although SI has a broader scope, privacy can only flourish in an environment where security is guaranteed.

We still have Artificial Intelligence (AI) governance where privacy is a central theme in the regulation of emerging technologies. AI, especially generative models like ChatGPT, introduces significant challenges related to people's privacy, algorithmic transparency, and accountability, such as state regulation, ethical principles, and the adoption of privacy-enhancing technologies (PETs).

Therefore, it is not just about understanding what needs to be done; it's about transforming principles into practices. My hope is that this book inspires you to delve deeper into this universe, exploring new technologies, improving processes or even rethinking the way you relate to data, systems and people.

Because in the end, privacy is not just a technical issue; It's a matter of respect, and it's up to all of us to ensure it is protected.

PREFACE

The accelerated digital transformation of recent years has brought unprecedented innovation, but it has also revealed a new reality: privacy and data protection have become indispensable elements in the development of any system. Regulations such as GDPR, LGPD and PDPL are no longer just legal requirements but have become an essential commitment to respecting users' rights.

However, for many developers and software engineers, implementing these concepts still seems like a complex and bureaucratic challenge.

It was with this scenario in mind that I wrote this book, based on my technical experience when dealing with privacy in real projects, where academic theory often proves insufficient to face the practical problems of everyday life. There is no more room to "add privacy later". The solution is to build it in from the beginning: privacy by design and by default.

Throughout the pages, my goal is to offer a straightforward and practical guide for IT professionals looking to understand how to implement privacy and data protection in practice. Each chapter has been structured so that you, as a software developer, engineer or architect, can immediately apply the techniques presented, with real examples and functional checklists. To make it easier to understand concepts that may seem distant or overly legal, I included stories inspired by real experiences, without exposing the names of the companies or people involved.

Although in some chapters I present excerpts of source code

or configurations, I do not intend to teach programming in this book, but only to provide a perspective on the technical feasibility of certain actions that can be performed.

With the pressure of regulations and tight deadlines, where priorities constantly change, many developers struggle to integrate privacy principles from the earliest stages of software design. Most technical teams still view privacy as a secondary concern, facing cultural barriers, lack of appropriate tools and the pressure for fast deliveries.

What is more critical, a security, usability or privacy bug?

Too often, organizational culture prioritizes functionality and speed of delivery over compliance and security, creating an environment where privacy is seen as an obstacle to innovation. Added to this is a significant awareness and training gap, where many developers lack a deep understanding of the ethical and legal implications of their design or architectural decisions. This misalignment between technical objectives and privacy expectations perpetuates reactive approaches that increase costs and risks throughout the software development lifecycle.

From the perspective of an IT project manager, cultural challenges related to privacy often arise from the difficulty in aligning business objectives with responsible technical practices. Managers face resistance from teams who see privacy as an obstacle to agility and innovation, especially in contexts where tight deadlines and quick deliveries predominate. The lack of clarity about responsibilities and priorities within the team can generate conflicts between the need to meet regulatory requirements and the pressure for functionalities and competitive advantages. Without an organizational culture that values privacy as a strategic pillar, the project manager finds himself challenged to balance technical feasibility, legal compliance and delivery objectives, often without adequate support or tools to integrate privacy into the project lifecycle.

If you're a developer, architect, or technical leader looking for clear, efficient ways to implement privacy, this book is for you. Privacy doesn't have to be an obstacle. When treated as a competitive differentiator, it can become a strong point that makes your software or company stand out in the market.

I want this book to encourage you to view privacy as more than regulations — an approach to building software that truly matters.

Let's start coding with privacy from the very first line.

CHAPTER 1

Technical Fundamentals of Privacy

Technical privacy represents the application of principles and practices aimed at protecting personal data within the scope of technology, ensuring that systems are designed and operated in a way that minimizes risks to users' privacy. Unlike merely conceptual or regulatory approaches, it is directly connected to technical decisions made during the software development life cycle and systems architecture. This includes everything from choosing anonymization and pseudonymization technologies to implementing access controls, activity monitoring, and data security in transit and at rest.

This concept encompasses good practices, frameworks and models that help technology teams implement privacy integrated into their routines. Solutions such as the use of zero trust architectures[1], designs guided by the principle of data minimization and automation of consent management processes are examples of how technical privacy manifests itself in everyday life. It's not just about protecting information, but about creating systems that, by default, respect individuals' privacy rights, allowing them to have control over how their data is collected, stored and used.

More than a set of tools, technical privacy demands a mindset that shapes every phase of a project. From initial requirements definition to systems operation and maintenance, teams must collaborate with privacy teams to align regulatory needs and strategic objectives with technical implementations. By adopting a privacy-by-design and privacy-by-default approach, developers, engineers, and architects not only meet ethical and security expectations, but also strengthen users' trust in the solutions they create.

Technology professionals with privacy expertise are able to:

- Plan data structures that guarantee the collection and storage of the minimum necessary personal information;
- Implement encryption and anonymization techniques for personal data;
- Use artificial intelligence solutions ethically and correctly in your systems;
- Develop components and functionalities in web pages and applications, respecting principles;
- Support technical infrastructure decisions, such as cloud hosting, data transit protection and secure storage policies;
- Apply secure development practices and privacy testing to critical projects.

The technical privacy professional goes beyond delivering a technological solution. He understands the challenges from a privacy and data protection perspective and proposes innovative solutions suitable for complex projects. In a world where APIs[2], components and systems are widely interconnected, this professional is essential for balancing technological innovation with regulatory compliance.

The increasing adoption of privacy regulations has created a highly supportive environment for professionals specializing in technical privacy. Companies of all sizes, in sectors such as finance, healthcare, retail and technology, are facing the urgent need to align their operations with these standards to avoid legal sanctions and preserve consumer trust. In this context, experts capable of incorporating privacy practices directly into the architecture and development of systems find an expanding market, with high demand for their skills.

This need goes beyond compliance, extending to the ability

for companies to differentiate themselves in the market by demonstrating a commitment to security and privacy.

Furthermore, the advancement of artificial intelligence, big data and cloud computing technologies is expanding opportunities for these professionals. The increasing complexity of systems requires solutions that not only meet legal requirements, but also address ethical concerns related to the collection and use of personal data and sensitive personal data. Technical privacy professionals are positioned as catalysts for responsible innovation, helping companies seize technological opportunities while mitigating risks associated with data breaches and information mismanagement. This balance between innovation and compliance transforms technical privacy into a strategic competency in the global market.

The accelerated advancement of artificial intelligence and the increasing use of technologies such as *deepfake*[3] they bring to light not only technical challenges, but also a vast field of opportunities in digital forensics. Technical privacy professionals with knowledge in forensic analysis and data security are in a privileged position to meet the growing demand for investigations related to fraud and cybercrime that use AI to create false identities, manipulate information and carry out scams of the most diverse types. These specialists can work on systems analysis, tracking malicious activities and validating data authenticity, being requested by justice bodies, auditing and security companies, as well as startups focused on anti-fraud technologies. The ability to understand and apply advanced privacy and security techniques, combined with forensic investigation skills, places these professionals at the forefront of a market that requires technical and judicial solutions to combat new forms of digital abuse.

A few years ago, even before GDPR became a real challenge for companies, I was in a meeting with a client, a large real estate company. It was year-end, and I saw that project as a promise of a comfortable Christmas with cash to spare.

The client did not skimp on requirements. He wanted something that today would be classified as "the perfect invasion of privacy manual". The idea was simple but bold: create a complete register of potential property buyers. And when I say complete, I really meant complete:

- Know how many properties they already owned;
- Integrate with registry databases (which, at that time, didn't even dream of having APIs);
- Do web scraping on search engines and social networks to create the buyer's profile, understand whether they could also be a potential seller and, thus, predict the best sales argument.

In other words, it was a project to ensure that the broker "spoke the same language" as the client, knew his personal tastes, knew the color of the car he wanted to buy and even the favorite song on the barbecue playlist. All this to generate a close and more "human" relationship (ironically, in a far from human way).

Excited, we started coming up with some ideas that would give privacy inspectors nightmares today. Even before Machine Learning was a buzzword, we developed ideas like:

- Identify relevant keywords in posts;
- Compare photos posted on social media to identify high-end properties;
- Map personal tastes based on public likes and interests;
- And even analyze the mood of posts to determine whether the buyer was in the mood to close a deal or just browsing the ads.

The client loved the idea, until we reached the budget. The project, bold as it was, was too expensive. So expensive that he chose to continue doing it the manual way: a few spreadsheets, a few calls here and there, and a lot of small talk to create rapport with buyers.

My Christmas? Simple, without big celebrations, but with a good dose of learning. After all, if that project had gotten off the ground, today we would all be subject to the severe consequences of privacy laws.

Moral of the story? Sometimes not approving a project can be the best decision for the future – and for your conscience. Today, looking back, I see how essential technical privacy is to balance innovation with ethics and respect for the user.

The global market for data privacy solutions has expanded rapidly in recent years. Recent estimates[4] indicate that the privacy software segment alone was valued at around US\$3.84 billion in 2024, with a forecast of reaching US\$45.13 billion by 2032 – which implies a CAGR (compound annual growth rate) of around 35%. Other studies[5] confirm this upward trend: for example, the privacy management software market was estimated at US\$3.41 billion in 2023 and is expected to grow by almost 40% per year until 2030.

The main drivers of this growth include the increase in data leakage incidents and cyber attacks – which lead companies to invest more in data protection – as well as greater consumer awareness about privacy, putting pressure on organizations to adopt more transparent and secure practices in the use of personal information.

Furthermore, regulatory pressure has intensified globally: more than 120 countries have already implemented national data protection laws by 2024 and governments around the world continue to strengthen citizens' privacy rights.

In response to this scenario, the market has seen an increasing adoption of "privacy by design" principles in the development of products and services, as well as the emergence of new technologies for compliance – for example, solutions that incorporate artificial intelligence to automate data protection and ensure regulatory compliance more efficiently

These combined trends have cemented privacy as one of the fastest-growing market segments in technology and data governance this decade, and technology professionals who are privacy experts have countless opportunities ahead of them.

In parallel with the market growth, there is a growing demand for professionals specialized in privacy. According to the International Association of Privacy Professionals (IAPP)[6], the demand for data privacy specialists has been increasing by around 30% per year, with many candidates receiving multiple job offers in a short period of time.

To meet this demand, professional certifications have become a valued standard on the resumes of privacy experts. The most recognized credentials globally are offered by IAPP itself – notably CIPP (Certified Information Privacy Professional), CIPM (Certified Information Privacy Manager) and CIPT (Certified Information Privacy Technologist) – which attest to knowledge in data protection laws, privacy program management and data protection by design techniques, respectively, in addition to other companies such as Exin, Isaca and ISC2 that have several certification programs in related areas.

In addition to professional associations, universities and international consultancy companies have been offering specialized programs (courses, MBAs and workshops) focused on privacy and data protection, indicating a global movement towards training to keep up with legal compliance requirements and the constant evolution of the privacy ecosystem.

In short, technical privacy isn't just a trend; it's a critical skill. It empowers technology professionals to implement robust solutions, respecting the rights of individuals and ensuring that privacy is present in every line of code, architecture and systems infrastructure.

PRIVACY
REGULATIONS

When I began writing this book, my goal was never to delve into overly academic details or explore the purely legal aspects of privacy laws. The literature on the topic is broad and well consolidated, offering analyzes of global regulations, their nuances and legal interpretations.

Privacy and data protection are complementary but distinct concepts, although both are recognized as fundamental rights in many jurisdictions. The main difference lies in its nature and scope of application: while privacy is a closed right, data protection is an open right, expansive and adaptable to new technological realities.

Privacy, in essence, is a closed right because it refers to a specific set of individual freedoms, such as the guarantee that people can control aspects of their personal lives and the exposure of information about themselves. It is the right to be left alone, to maintain confidentiality in private communications and to avoid undue interference in one's personal life. This right is more static and strongly associated with human dignity, protecting the person's intimate spheres against external intrusions.

Data protection is an open right, as it goes beyond privacy and covers the governance of personal data in a digitalized world. It involves control over how a person's data is collected, processed, stored and shared, regardless of whether it is related to the private or public sphere. Data protection is dynamic, adapting to technological changes and new uses of personal information in scenarios such as artificial intelligence, big data and the digital economy.

> *"Recent inventions and new methods of business call attention to the next step that must be taken to protect the person and to secure to the individual what Judge Cooley calls the right "to be let alone." Instant photographs and journalistic activity invaded the sacred domains of private and domestic life; and countless mechanical devices threaten to realize the prediction that "what is whispered in the bedroom will be proclaimed from the housetops." There has been a perception for years that the law must provide some remedy for the unauthorized circulation of portraits of private individuals; and the problem of invasion of privacy by newspapers, long felt keenly, was recently discussed by a renowned writer. The facts alleged in a notorious case brought to a lower New York court a few months ago directly involved the question of the circulation of portraits; and the question of whether our legislation will recognize and protect the right to privacy in this and other respects must soon be considered by our courts.*
>
> *"* [7]

Both are fundamental rights because they guarantee the dignity and autonomy of individuals in a connected society. Privacy safeguards respect for the personal sphere and individual freedom, while data protection enables individuals to control their information across diverse contexts, such as commercial relationships, digital services and government interactions.

Joana was an architect passionate about plants, but very reserved about her personal life. When he bought a new house, the first thing he did was install thick curtains and security cameras. Curtains protect your privacy: they ensure that no one from the outside can observe what happens inside your home, preserving your privacy. Cameras, on the other hand, protected your property and recorded who entered or left, ensuring that any access was controlled and monitored.

One day, Joana decided to share photos of the garden she was cultivating on her favorite social network. She allowed everyone to see the flowers and the progress of her project, but was careful not to post images that showed the inside of the house. Privacy, in this case, was like the space that the curtains still protect: even when sharing something, she chose what remained invisible. However, photos of the garden contained location information that she didn't notice, such as the street name captured on a sign in the background. This is where data protection came into play: The social network should guarantee that this information isn't misused or shared without her consent.

Thus, Joana learned that privacy was the right to decide what was visible or hidden in her life, while data protection dealt with how the information she chose to share was treated. The two things go together, but they have different roles. One is control over what she wants to expose; the other is the guarantee that what has been exposed will be treated with respect and safety.

In short, privacy is the historical and conceptual foundation, while data protection expands this right to respond to the contemporary challenges of digital society.

Both, when complementing each other, form a set of guarantees that preserve individual fundamental rights in an increasingly data-driven world.

> "In any case, understanding the scope of protection of a fundamental right to the protection of personal data always involves a contrast with that of other rights, highlighting, in this context, the right to privacy and the right to informational self-determination, which, in turn, although also autonomous from each other, present important contact zones."[8]

However, for the technical privacy professional, the most important thing is to understand the fundamental principles that underlie these regulations through these concepts and, mainly, how they directly influence decisions and day-to-day technical activities.

Consider a practical example: you use a database hosted in a Microsoft Azure private cloud in the United States and your company is expanding operations to Germany. In this scenario, what adjustments to the infrastructure and scalability of the system would be necessary to meet the most stringent requirements for international data transfer? What once seemed like a simple software architecture decision can turn into a global review, requiring not only technical compliance, but also strategies for dealing with different jurisdictions and regulations, reducing or transferring the organization's risk.

> "OpenAI has launched a data residency option in Europe, enabling European organizations to meet local data sovereignty requirements while utilizing the company's AI products. Data residency refers to the physical location of an organization's data, as well as the local laws and policy requirements imposed on that data. Most major technology companies and cloud providers offer data residency programs in Europe, helping customers comply with local privacy and data protection laws such as GDPR, the German Federal Data Protection Act and UK data protection legislation. In October, development platform GitHub launched the EU cloud data residency option for customers subscribing to the GitHub Enterprise plan. In the same month, Amazon's cloud computing division AWS launched a "sovereign cloud" for Europe, allowing customers to keep all metadata they create within the EU, while Google introduced data residency for machine learning processing for UK users using the Gemini 1.5 Flash AI model."[9]

Imagine new regulations are introduced, changing the rules

for data in transit and at rest. How do these changes affect your organization's business continuity plan (BCP)? The high availability of systems, essential to avoid operational interruptions, can be compromised if there are no clear criteria and technical adaptability to incorporate these new requirements. Situations like these show how privacy is not just a regulatory issue, but also a strategic and technical challenge that requires planning, flexibility and execution.

Additionally, changes to supplementary guidelines such as ePrivacy[10] in the European Union, they can have profound impacts on web systems and digital marketing strategies.

The question then arises: Are your current integrations and APIs prepared to adapt to new global demands? Something seemingly simple, like how to implement cookies, manage user tracking or run automated email campaigns, can require a complete overhaul, from infrastructure to operational processes.

These questions highlight an important point: they only arise with in-depth technical knowledge about how systems work. This level of understanding, however, often escapes professionals who work exclusively in the legal or regulatory sphere. During data flow mapping, architectural and technical nuances often go unnoticed by those who were not directly involved in the design and implementation of the systems.

This is where the role of the technical privacy professional becomes essential. This professional understands the details that support systems architecture, from the way data is captured and stored to how it travels across networks and interacts with APIs. His expertise is the link that connects regulatory requirements with technical feasibility, ensuring that solutions meet not only standards, but also expectations for efficiency, security and scalability.

Although the landscape is constantly evolving, currently the most significant regulations include:

The GDPR (General Data Protection Regulation), which is one of the broadest and most stringent data protection regulations. Created by the European Union, it sets out clear rules on how EU citizens' personal data should be collected, stored, processed and shared. It also grants individuals significant rights, such as the right to access, rectify and delete their data, and imposes heavy fines on organizations that fail to comply.

The LGPD (General Data Protection Law) is the main data protection legislation in Brazil, heavily inspired by the GDPR. It regulates the processing of personal data, requiring organizations to respect the purposes of data processing in addition to ensuring transparency about how this information is processed. The LGPD also grants Brazilian citizens rights such as access, correction and deletion of their data, in addition to establishing penalties for violations.

The CPPA (Consumer Privacy Protection Act) came into force in 2023 replacing PIPEDA. It offers similar rights to the GDPR, such as the right to access and rectify data, and imposes stricter obligations on organizations, including the need to notify data breaches.

India's Digital Personal Data Protection Act (DPDP), passed in 2023, replaces the previous framework based on the Information Technology Act, 2000 and the Personal Data Protection Bill (PDPB), 2019. The new legislation establishes modern guidelines for the protection of personal data, aligning with international practices.

PECR (Privacy and Electronic Communications Regulations) is the UK version of the EU ePrivacy directive, which remains in force even after Brexit[11]. It regulates the use of cookies, electronic marketing and confidential communications, requiring explicit consent for activities such as online tracking. PECR complements GDPR in the UK, focusing specifically on electronic communications.

POPIA (Protection of Personal Information Act) is the main data protection legislation in South Africa. It regulates the collection, processing and storage of personal data, requiring organizations to obtain consent and ensure the security of information. POPIA also grants individuals rights such as data access and correction, as well as establishing penalties for violations.

The APEC Privacy Framework is a set of guidelines aimed at protecting data in countries in the Asia-Pacific region. It promotes principles such as harm prevention, notification and consent, aiming to harmonize privacy practices among APEC members. Although not a binding law, the framework influences national policies and regulations in the region.

PIPL (Personal Information Protection Law) is the first Chinese law specifically dedicated to the protection of personal data. It establishes clear rules about how data should be collected, stored and processed, requiring explicit consent and limiting the use of personal data. PIPL represents China's growing concern for data privacy and security, partially aligning with global standards such as GDPR.

PDPL (Personal Data Protection Law) is personal data protection legislation adopted by several countries, including Saudi Arabia, Peru and Taiwan. In Saudi Arabia, PDPL is regulated by the Saudi Arabian Data and Artificial Intelligence Authority (SDAIA) and imposes specific requirements for data operations within the country, including restrictions on international data transfer except under specific conditions. In Peru, legislation is overseen by the General Data Protection Agency, while in Taiwan, ministries and local government bodies act as competent authorities.

As of the date of publication of this work, currently, 71% of countries in the world have specific legislation on the protection of personal data, which is equivalent to approximately 134 nations[12]. Furthermore, 9% of countries have bills in the approval phase, while 15% do not yet have legislation on the topic. Europe stands out with 98% of countries adopting data protection legislation, followed by the Americas with 74% and the Asia-Pacific region with 57%.

In the United States, the approach to privacy is fragmented, without general federal legislation. Instead, the country adopts a sectoral model, where different laws regulate specific sectors, such as health, finance and children. This system creates a decentralized regulatory landscape, often resulting in protection gaps and inconsistencies across states and sectors.

Among the main laws in the USA are:

- Electronic Communications Privacy Act (ECPA) (1986): regulates interception and access to electronic communications.
- Children's Online Privacy Protection Act (COPPA) (1998): protects the privacy of children under 13 online.
- Health Insurance Portability and Accountability Act (HIPAA) (1996): establishes rules for the privacy and security of health data.
- Privacy Act (1974): regulates the processing of personal information by federal agencies.

Additionally, the California Consumer Privacy Act (CCPA) of 2018 is an example of state legislation that provides broad rights to consumers, including access, deletion, and opt-out of the sale of personal data.

The CCPA was one of the first privacy and data protection laws in the United States. It gives California residents the right to know what personal data is being collected about them, how that data is used, and with whom it is shared. Additionally, it allows consumers to request the deletion of their data and opt out of having it sold. The CCPA was an important milestone for privacy in the US, inspiring other state legislation.

The CPRA (California Privacy Rights Act) is an amendment to the CCPA that further strengthens privacy protections in California.

It introduces additional rights, such as the ability to correct inaccurate data and limit the use of data related to a person, such as precise location, race and health. The CPRA also created a new agency dedicated to privacy oversight, increasing enforcement of the rules.

The absence of a National Data Protection Authority, as in the European model, makes the application of these rules more fragmented, being the responsibility of different regulatory bodies, such as the Federal Trade Commission (FTC) and the Department of Health and Human Services.

The decision of the Court of Justice of the European Union in the Schrems II case[13] invalidated the Privacy Shield, a mechanism that allowed data transfer between the EU and the US, highlighting the lack of adequate guarantees for the protection of data of European citizens in the US.

The Schrems II Case

The Schrems II case was a milestone in data protection between the European Union and the United States. In 2020, the Court of Justice of the European Union invalidated Privacy Shield, an agreement that allowed the transfer of personal data from European citizens to the US. The decision originated in a lawsuit filed by Austrian activist Max Schrems, who questioned the security of European data when stored in American territory, especially in light of US surveillance laws, such as FISA (Foreign Intelligence Surveillance Act).

The court's central argument was that Privacy Shield did not offer sufficient guarantees to protect Europeans' data against mass surveillance by American agencies. Companies in the US were subject to allowing the government access to personal information without offering European citizens an effective means of rebuttal or legal protections equivalent to those guaranteed by the GDPR. The ruling not only invalidated the Privacy Shield, but also required European companies to

---

review their data transfer practices to ensure compliance with European standards.

The impact of the decision was immediate, forcing thousands of companies to look for alternatives, such as the use of standard contractual clauses, to continue transferring data between continents. The Schrems II case also boosted negotiations for a new data transfer agreement, leading to the development of the Data Privacy Framework, which seeks to meet the requirements of European legislation. However, the ruling continues to influence the global debate on data sovereignty and the challenges of harmonizing privacy regulations across different jurisdictions.

As can be seen, each country or region has its own regulations with distinct characteristics: some with more expansionist and protective approaches, others with a more permissive bias and focusing on innovation and economic growth. However, the main objective is the same: to regulate how public and private companies treat people's data, ensuring transparency, security and respect for the right to privacy.

PRIVACY STANDARDS AND FRAMEWORKS

To operate globally, a technical manager or software engineer needs to have a solid understanding of several areas that transcend coding and systems development. Firstly, it is worth knowing the privacy and data protection regulations at an international level, such as the ones I brought as an example, in addition to understanding their intersections and differences to ensure compliance in global projects. This includes studying the fundamental principles of these laws, such as data minimization, consent, transparency and data subject rights. Furthermore, it is important to stay up to date with legislative changes and new regulatory requirements in different regions, which requires a continuous learning effort.

On the technical side, these professionals must delve deeper into practices such as Privacy by Design[14] and Privacy by Default, advanced encryption techniques, anonymization, tokenization and security frameworks to ensure that developed systems meet privacy requirements by design. Knowledge in information security, such as preventing data leaks and protecting against cyber attacks, is essential. Furthermore, it is important to develop skills in agile methodologies and DevSecOps[15], integrating compliance testing and privacy auditing into the software development lifecycle. In addition, it is essential to invest in *soft skills*, such as intercultural communication and collaboration, which are essential for dealing with multidisciplinary teams and clients in a diverse global environment.

In addition to regulations, there are technical standards and frameworks that complement and reinforce privacy program strategies. These technical guides help cut through the legalese and dive into practical work with development and infrastructure teams.

Among the most relevant are:

ePrivacy is a European regulation that complements the GDPR, focusing specifically on privacy issues related to electronic communications. It addresses topics such as the use of cookies, digital tracking and direct marketing, requiring companies to obtain explicit consent from users before collecting or processing data in these situations, where applicable. ePrivacy aims to ensure that online communications are confidential and that users have control over how their information is used.

OWASP (Application Security Verification Standard) is a set of practices and standards aimed at the security and privacy of web applications. It includes specific recommendations on handling cookies, protecting against data leaks, and mitigating common vulnerabilities. OWASP is widely used by developers and security teams to ensure that web applications are built with privacy and security from the start.

The NIST Privacy Framework is a framework developed by the US National Institute of Standards and Technology to help organizations manage privacy risks in technology systems. It provides practical guidelines for implementing the concept of Privacy by Design, ensuring that privacy is considered at every stage of product and service development. The framework is adaptable and can be applied in different sectors and contexts.

The W3C Web Privacy Standards are technical standards created by the World Wide Web Consortium to improve privacy on the web. They include solutions such as Do Not Track (DNT), which allows users to opt out of being tracked, and P3P (Platform for Privacy Preferences), which facilitates the communication of privacy policies between websites and browsers. These standards aim to give users more control over their online data.

By the way, the W3C's Do Not Track (DNT) concept is an initiative that aims to offer users a way to express their preference not to have their web activities tracked by websites and advertisers. This preference is communicated through an HTTP header sent by the browser when accessing a page. When the feature is enabled, the header informs servers that the user prefers their browsing behavior not to be monitored. This mechanism seeks to address privacy concerns by allowing users to have greater control over how their data is collected and used.

Implementing DNT requires changes on both the browser side and the server side. Browsers must include the functionality to enable header sending, while servers must be configured to recognize this preference and adjust data collection behavior accordingly. While the concept is technically feasible, its effectiveness depends on organizations voluntarily adhering to the header and implementing clear, verifiable do-not-track policies.

To implement Do Not Track (DNT) on a web system, a developer can configure the backend to detect and respect the HTTP header DNT, which browsers send when the user activates this option. In practice, this means modifying the site's data collection logic to check for the presence of this header and adjusting the behavior of the user tracking system.

On the backend, an HTTP server can inspect incoming requests and, if the header DNT: 1 is present, prevent the activation of tracking scripts, browsing data logging or any other monitoring mechanism. In a web application developed with Node.js, for example, middleware in Express can be used to block tracking cookies and other monitoring practices:

Just as an example, see what a Node.js code would look like with Express to respect DNT.

```javascript
// Example in Node.js with Express to respect DNT
const express = require('express');
const app = express();

app.use((req, res, next) => {
  if (req.get('DNT') === '1') {
    console.log('Tracking disabled for this user.');
    res.set('Tk', 'N'); // Indicates that tracking has been disabled
    // Prevent execution of analytics scripts
  } else {
    // Default tracking logic
  }
  next();
});
```

On the frontend, JavaScript can be configured to prevent tracking scripts from running if the DNT header is enabled in the browser. A check can be done using the navigator.doNotTrack API:

Additionally, if your application uses third-party services for collecting metrics, advertising, or user analytics, you must verify that those services support DNT and provide specific instructions for disabling tracking when the header is detected.

In practice, DNT has encountered significant barriers. Many companies have not adopted the standard or explicitly stated how they would handle user-submitted preferences. Furthermore, without robust auditing or regulatory mechanisms, DNT has remained more of a symbolic initiative than a widely accepted solution to online privacy issues. Even so, it served as a starting point for discussions about privacy.

ENISA (European Union Agency for Cybersecurity) is a European Union agency that defines guidelines to ensure security and privacy in communication networks. It provides recommendations on how to protect data in transit, prevent breaches, and implement robust security measures. ENISA also helps promote good privacy and security practices across the EU.

The IAB Europe Transparency and Consent Framework (TCF) is a standard developed by Interactive Advertising Bureau Europe to promote transparency and consent in digital marketing and online advertising. It sets out clear rules about how user data can be collected and used for advertising purposes, ensuring users have control over their privacy preferences. The TCF is widely adopted by advertising and technology companies as it is a framework designed to help companies meet the privacy and consent requirements imposed by regulations such as GDPR and ePrivacy. It is relevant for developers working on applications that involve digital advertising, data collection, or integration with ad platforms. Its main objective is to provide transparency about how user data is collected, stored and processed, as well as ensuring that the necessary consents are obtained and managed appropriately.

For a developer, TCF requires attention to some essential aspects. The implementation involves the integration of a CMP (Consent Management Platform), which serves to capture, manage and transmit users' consent preferences in a standardized way. The developer must ensure that the CMP is configured correctly, following the TCF technical specifications, including the use of APIs and communication methods to record user consent and pass it on to involved partners, such as ad networks or technology providers.

The developer needs to be concerned about the system's compatibility with TCF requirements, especially regarding the capture and storage of consent choices. This includes ensuring that consent is granular (allowing the user to choose which purposes they authorize) and verifiable, to ensure legal compliance. It must also be observed that the data collected respects the limits defined by the user's consent, which may imply adjustments in the backend to restrict data processing.

Clients that frequently require the use of TCF include companies involved in programmatic advertising, such as online content publishers, marketing agencies, ad management platforms, and data providers. These customers rely on TCF to ensure their operations comply with privacy regulations while maintaining the ability to monetize their content and services.

So in practice, if you need to implement TCF:

1. Choose an IAB-certified CMP or develop your own solution;
2. Add CMP script to manage consent;
3. Store user preferences in localStorage or use the CMP API;
4. Share TC String with advertising providers to ensure ads respect user choices;
5. Control the execution of consent-based tracking scripts. Update privacy policy for transparency.

The EFF Privacy Badger Guidelines are guidelines developed by the Electronic Frontier Foundation (EFF) to combat abusive tracking on digital platforms. Privacy Badger is a browser extension that automatically blocks invisible trackers and third-party cookies that monitor users' behavior without their consent. The EFF guidelines emphasize the importance of protecting users' privacy and promoting transparency in online tracking.

These already established standards are important, in addition to several institutions, corporations and independent organizations that are constantly working to improve solutions that:

- Strengthen digital security;
- Protect users' privacy;
- And promote safer and more transparent environments for everyone;
- Are aligned with the company's privacy program.

In addition to market standards, it is important that professionals closely monitor trends, initiatives from companies and groups that frequently publish new developments in the area. One of these initiatives is "Privacy Patterns"[16].

Privacy Patterns is an initiative that brings together a library of design patterns aimed at protecting privacy in software systems. The platform was created to help developers, software engineers and designers incorporate privacy practices from the conception of systems, following the concept of "Privacy by Design".

The standards provided provide solutions to common privacy-related issues, such as data anonymization, access control, transparency about the use of personal information, and consent management. Each standard includes detailed descriptions, usage examples, and guidance on how to apply them, making them a practical tool for implementing privacy requirements.

The initiative is maintained by privacy experts, academics and professionals in the technology sector who seek to promote the development of more ethical and user-centered systems. Privacy Patterns' work is especially relevant for companies that want to improve their approach to privacy and for teams that need to design secure and reliable technological solutions. By offering accessible and well-documented resources, the platform facilitates the adoption of best privacy practices in different types of projects, from web applications to complex corporate systems, helping to strengthen user trust and reduce legal risks associated with the misuse of personal data.

If you have to study each standard it will take time, so, as I have already done this, I present below a summary of the main privacy standards and my vision on their implementation, but you need to adapt each scenario to your reality.

A principle that stands out in privacy is minimizing the data collected and exposed. The pattern **"Location Granularity"** illustrates this by suggesting that services collect or disclose only the necessary location accuracy, avoiding excessive detail. For example, a weather app might just use the address or city instead of the exact GPS coordinate, maintaining functionality and reducing the risk of accurate identification or malicious use of the data.

In a similar way, **"Protection against Tracking"** prevents user tracking by limiting third-party cookies – deleting them regularly or blocking them by default – which makes it difficult to build complete browsing profiles about the individual. This pattern, common in browsers with anti-tracking settings or extensions such as cookie blockers, protects the user from invasive profiling and targeting.

Another example of minimization is **"Strip Invisible Metadata"**, which removes hidden metadata from files (for example, stripping EXIF data from photo locations) to prevent disclosure of information embedded in the content. Some platforms already apply this standard, preventing details such as GPS coordinates or device identity from accompanying a shared file.

In certain scenarios, instead of eliminating data, inaccuracy can be added in a controlled way: **"Added-noise measurement obfuscation"** introduces statistical noise into the collected data, masking individual values without compromising overall trends. This technique, used in differential privacy by large companies to collect statistics, significantly reduces the risk of re-identifying users from aggregated data sets - We will talk even more about anonymization techniques later.

To protect the user's identity, several standards focus on anonymity and breaking tracking links. THE **"Onion Routing"** is a classic traffic anonymization pattern: it encapsulates communications in multiple layers of encryption and routes them through multiple nodes, so that no intermediary knows both the origin and the final destination. The Tor network (The Onion Router) exemplifies this concept, guaranteeing a high degree of privacy – external observers are unable to associate the user with the websites they access.

Another pattern, **"Anonymity Set"**, dilutes each individual into a larger group to hide it in the crowd. Only aggregated data from at least a certain number k of users is disclosed, ensuring that no single record identifies anyone (k-anonymity concept).

In the same effort to confuse possible vigilantes, **"Use of dummies"** adds fake actions or data mixed in with real ones, making it difficult for third parties to distinguish true user behaviors. For example, a privacy-compromised search app could trigger additional random queries beyond those searched by the user, scrambling any attempt to profile the user.

Similarly, the **"Identity Federation Do Not Track Pattern"** prevents centralized identity providers (such as social networks used for login) from monitoring all services where the user authenticates. Architectures inspired by this pattern (for example, federated login with anonymous intermediaries or "Sign in with Apple"-style "aliased emails") ensure that the identity provider does not know which sites the user has entered, nor do these sites know unnecessary information about the user. In short, these patterns of anonymization and identity dissociation make it extremely difficult to link online actions to a specific person, strengthening privacy and preventing widespread tracking.

In addition to complete anonymity, there are situations in which it is desirable to use alternative identities or minimize revealed attributes. The pattern **"Pseudonymous Identity"** advocates allowing users to interact using identifiers that do not refer to their real identity – such as nicknames or secondary accounts – so that their activities are not directly linked to their real name. This is common on forums and networks where the individual prefers privacy: even if data from that account is leaked, it does not reveal the person behind it.

In the same vein, **"Pseudonymous Messaging"** allows communication through pseudonyms or trusted intermediaries, hiding the real sender and recipient. Anonymous remailer services or disposable emails illustrate this practice, useful for complaints or sensitive discussions, as they enable contact without exposing identities.

Already **"Masquerade"** goes a step further by letting the user provide deliberately altered or filtered information to a service. A simple example is using an alternative email address for registrations – this way, the user's main email remains protected, and if that alias is spammed or leaked, it can be discarded without prejudice.

Finally, about anonymization, **"Attribute Based Credentials"** introduces a form of selective authentication: instead of revealing their full identity, the user only presents credentials for specific attributes. For example, you can prove that you are of legal age using a cryptographic token, without exposing your name or date of birth. This standard reconciles functionality with privacy, guaranteeing requirements (such as verifying age or license) with minimal disclosure of personal data.

Ensuring user autonomy over their data starts with obtaining consent. **"Obtaining Explicit Consent"** and **"Lawful Consent"** ensure that no personal data is processed without clear and valid acceptance from the holder. In practice, this involves presenting well-defined opt-in options (for example, unchecked checkboxes that the user must actively select) accompanied by understandable information about what will be done with the data – fulfilling the criteria of free, informed, specific and unambiguous consent required by privacy laws.

"Informed Implicit Consent" complements this by dealing with cases in which the use of the service implies tacit consent: even in these cases, the system must prominently warn the user about what is being consented to. A banner stating "By continuing to browse, you agree to analysis cookies" is one example – ensuring the user is aware of the implied agreement. Additionally, if data is transferred to third parties, the standard **"Outsourcing [with consent]"** recommends obtaining extra, specific consent before involving external partners in processing information. Thus, the user is not surprised by shares beyond the entity to which they initially granted the data. Of course, you need to pay attention to the specific criteria of your regulation - Depending on the region or the type of personal data, informed consent without positive action from the user is not enough.

The standards also ensure that, after initial consent, the user maintains fine-grained control over what they share, when, and with whom. A central approach is **"Selective Disclosure"**, in which the service adapts to the data that the user is willing to provide. Instead of requiring a complete package of information, the system works even if the user chooses not to fill in everything – perhaps with limited functionality, but without blocking access. For example, if a form asks for a telephone number and address but the user only provides their email address, registration still continues. In that same spirit of flexibility, **"Enable/Disable Functions"** offers switches for features that involve personal data, allowing the user to activate or deactivate functionalities such as geolocation, activity history or advertising personalization according to their preference. This way, he can take advantage of the service by adjusting the areas he considers invasive, instead of having to accept everything or nothing. In the same way, **"Selective access control"** and the concept of **"Buddy List"** ensure that the user chooses the audience for each information they share. The platform can, by default, isolate shares to a restricted circle of friends or trusted contacts, and let the user manually expand the audience if desired.

To be **"Reasonable Level of Control"** – select recipients or groups for each post, photo or data – avoids unnecessary exposure, keeping the different spheres of the user's life separate. Additionally, **"Active broadcast of presence"** proposes to give control over online status: the user could decide when to notify his contacts of his presence (for example, manually turning on an "available" indicator), instead of the system automatically showing everyone when he is connected.

To avoid slips, **"Discouraging blanket strategies"** suggests not applying single global settings to every activity. Instead, the interface invites the user to choose the level of privacy with each new publication or share – for example, confirming whether that specific item will be public, friends only or restricted – which prevents forgetting an open setting that exposes future content. And if the user makes a mistake, **"Preventing mistakes or reducing their impact"** implements safeguards: confirmation prompts before irreversible actions (such as submitting sensitive information), post-submission editing or removal options, or regret periods ("undo" a post immediately after publishing).

Already the **"Decoupling content and location information visibility"** deals with a specific but important case: it allows location information attached to content to be hidden or removed independently of the content itself. So, if a user initially shared a geotagged photo but later reconsiders, they can remove the location without having to delete the entire photo, granting retroactive control over contextual data. As the user uses the system, their preferences can be gradually refined – an idea captured in the standard **"Negotiation of Privacy Policy"**, which proposes adjusting privacy settings over time based on the user's own choices and feedback.

Some standards focus on aligning the interests of the user and the system, offering benefits to encourage conscious sharing. **"Reciprocity"** suggests that users receive value proportional to the data contributions they make – for example, by providing information they gain access to aggregated analysis or data from others in return. **"Pay Back"** emphasizes direct rewards such as discounts, bonuses or extra features in exchange for personal information or content provided. Already **"Incentivized Participation"** combines these ideas, indicating that users collaborate more when they see a fair return or when the contribution can be made anonymously and securely. The advantage of these standards is to increase users' willingness to share useful data: they do so because they see utility or fairness in the exchange (be it a financial, social or informational benefit), while at the same time their privacy expectations are met.

Transparency about data practices is important. **"Privacy Policy Display"** recommends clearly informing, at the time of collection, why personal data is requested and how it will be used, reducing information asymmetry (according to the standard **"Minimal Information Asymmetry"** seeks to do). For example, next to a phone number field may be the note "Used for delivery notifications only." **"Dynamic Privacy Policy Display"** takes this into real-time context, providing explanations through tooltips or informative media exactly when the user interacts with a privacy-related field, eliminating doubts at the right time.

Even so, full policies are often long; that's why, **"Layered Policy Design"** organizes terms into layers: first a short, friendly summary with key points, followed by expandable sections with full legal details. Similarly, **"Abridged Terms and Conditions"** provides a summarized version of the terms of use, highlighting important clauses in an accessible way. Visual techniques also help with transparency: **"Privacy Labels"** proposes a standardized table that summarizes categories of collected data and their use, similar to a nutritional label, allowing you to easily compare services.

Furthermore, **"Privacy icons"**, together with **"Icons for Privacy Policies"** and **"Appropriate Privacy Icons"**, advocates the use of universal symbols to represent aspects of policy (for example, a padlock icon to indicate protected data, or a third-party arrow figure to indicate external sharing). The pattern **"Privacy Color Coding"** complements it with colors indicating privacy levels (green for private information, yellow for restrictedly shared, red for public, for example). Finally, **"Privacy Aware Wording"** remember that the language of explanations must be simple and engaging, avoiding technical or legal jargon that could be confusing. Together, these presentation and writing standards make privacy policies much more understandable, increasing the likelihood that the user truly understands what they are consenting to.

It is also worth mentioning the efforts to standardize preferences and privacy policies. THE **"Platform for Privacy Preferences"** (P3P) defined a format for websites to publish their policies in a machine-readable form, and the standard **"Policy Matching Display"** provided that browsers or user agents would compare these policies with the user's personal preferences, alerting them to incompatibilities.

One **"Privacy-Aware Network Client"** – essentially a privacy-aware browser or plug-in – could, for example, automatically read a website's policy and indicate whether it meets or violates preferences a user has set (such as honoring a "Do Not Track" request). In practice, these approaches have faced adoption challenges and have not become widely popular, but they represent important attempts to automate transparency and align service policies with users' stated expectations.

Keeping users aware of how and when their data is used over time is equally important. **"Asynchronous notice"** recommends periodically notifying users of continued access to their data after initial consent. For example, an app might remind the user that they have accessed their location 20 times in the last week, giving them a chance to review that permission. **"Ambient Notice"** prefers subtle, immediate warnings during use – such as a small icon or light turning on whenever the camera or microphone is active – so that the user has real-time awareness of ongoing monitoring.

Other patterns provide more explicit feedback: **"Who's Listening"** shows the user exactly who (other users or parties) viewed or has access to a certain content of theirs, giving an idea of audience and reach. **"Impactful Information and Feedback"** it goes further by warning in advance about the possible consequences of sharing something – for example, indicating before sending a post how widely it will be disseminated. Already **"Appropriate Privacy Feedback"** covers all post-action feedback that the system must clearly provide, such as confirming that data was shared with a certain party or warning when user information is accessed by third parties.

Patterns like **"Privacy Awareness Panel"** or **"Awareness Feed"** insert fixed elements or historical feeds into the interface that keep the user aware of privacy-related events – for example, a section showing "Recent activity: your profile has been viewed 3 times today" or remembering relevant current settings ("Your public profile currently displays your last access"). Furthermore, **"Increasing awareness of information aggregation"** emphasizes educating the user about how seemingly isolated data can, when combined, reveal identity or other data related to the person. Warnings or tutorials can illustrate that filling out multiple optional fields at different times allows for non-obvious correlations, encouraging more caution. Altogether, these continuous notification and feedback mechanisms ensure that the user is not left in the dark after providing consent and can proactively monitor and adjust their choices.

In addition to warnings and feedback, offer tools for the user to directly inspect and manage their data. **"Privacy dashboard"** calls a central dashboard where the user can view what personal data the service has collected and is storing, as well as adjust privacy preferences in one place. Several platforms already have panels like this, showing search history, activities, connected apps, and allowing you to revoke permissions or delete records easily. In the same sense, **"Personal Data Table"** refers to providing, on demand, a detailed inventory of all data that the controller holds about the user – often as part of the right of access guaranteed by law. This may come in the form of a report or downloadable file containing profile information, usage records, logs, etc. **"Privacy Mirrors"**, in turn, reflect back to the user the system's view of him: they reveal what information about him is stored, what inferences or profiles were generated from this data, and which entities had access. This total transparency allows the user to see whether the digital image he projects meets his expectations and, if necessary, request corrections or removals. By making these introspection resources available – control panel, personal data table, privacy mirror – the organization empowers the user to monitor and make informed decisions about their data throughout its lifecycle in the system.

Within architecture and internal processes, several standards enforce privacy and compliance without direct user interaction. **"Encryption with user-managed keys"** is an example: personal data is stored end-to-end encrypted, and only the user holds the keys to decrypt it. Therefore, not even the service provider can read the content – an approach adopted by secure email services and some cloud systems, which protects confidentiality even in the event of a server hack or legal data requirement (as the provider is unable to provide readable text). **"Single Point of Contact"** is a security standard that centralizes all requests for access to sensitive data in a single authorizing entity. Instead of each subsystem accessing sensitive data directly, it passes through this control point that validates credentials and applies uniform policies, reducing the chance of unauthorized access and facilitating audits.

On the other hand, **"User data confinement pattern"** and

"Personal Data Store" adopt the philosophy of keeping as much data as possible under the user's own control – whether processing locally on the user's device or storing data in a personal repository controlled by the user. Only strictly necessary data is sent to central servers. This separation minimizes the amount of information exposed in centralized bases that can be targets of attack. **"Aggregation Gateway"** it also limits exposure: data from multiple users is encrypted and aggregated by an intermediary before it goes to the final service, so that the server only receives collective statistics rather than raw individual data.

The standard **"Trustworthy Privacy Plug-in"** proposes to include a local component – typically on the client side – responsible for reliably aggregating and recording usage events, sharing only filtered or anonymized results with the server. This allows certain analyzes (such as usage metrics) to be done on the user's device, under their supervision, increasing confidence that their raw data will not be leaked. In terms of policies, **"Obligation Management"** ensures that obligations associated with data (e.g. retention period, prohibition on transfer) are met even when data circulates across different systems. Related to this, the idea of **"Sticky Policies"** is to attach machine-readable policies to data so that any receiving system knows and is technically compelled to respect the restrictions and obligations set by the original controller or subject.

"Sign an Agreement to Solve Lack of Trust on the Use of Private Data", has a big name and addresses legal responsibility: it suggests that the service provider sign formal agreements committing to limit the use of data to specific purposes and to protect user privacy, creating an additional contractual obligation beyond mere consent. In addition to this, **"Trust Evaluation of Services Sides"** introduces independent audits and certifications that assess the level of privacy of a service – the equivalent of a seal of quality in data protection, which can be displayed to the public.

Finally, **"Federated Privacy Impact Assessment"** recommends that when multiple parties or organizations share data (such as in federated systems or partner integrations), a comprehensive privacy impact assessment be conducted considering the entire ecosystem. This anticipates emerging risks from correlating data between disparate sources and helps mitigate privacy issues that would only manifest when previously separate systems begin exchanging information. All of these internal standards work behind the scenes to ensure that the system protects data in accordance with privacy principles, even beyond direct user interaction.

Despite all precautions, it is necessary to be prepared for incidents and take care of user safety. **"Data Breach Notification Pattern"** establishes that, in the event of a personal data breach, the organization must quickly detect the problem and notify regulatory authorities and impacted users without delay. This allows holders to take protective measures (such as changing passwords or being alert to fraud attempts) and demonstrates transparency and responsibility on the part of the service, mitigating damage to trust. Already **"Unusual Activities"** is a preventive standard that monitors access and behavior in search of anomalies that may indicate misuse or account hacking. For example, login attempts from unusual locations or access at unusual times may trigger alerts, request additional two-factor authentication, or temporarily block the account until confirmed.

In the context of online communities, **"Anonymous Reputation-based Blacklisting"** allows you to ban malicious users based on reputation or anonymous identifiers, without requiring to know their real identity. A forum might, for example, assign fixed tokens or pseudonyms to anonymous contributors and block those with a history of abuse, while legitimate participants remain protected by anonymity. Finally, the user authentication layer is also covered: **"Informed Secure**

Passwords" encourages the design of registration and login interfaces that educate the user about good password practices – indicating real-time password strength, or warning if a chosen password has already appeared in known leaks – helping to prevent weak accounts that would compromise privacy. AND **"Informed Credential Selection"** suggests that when multiple ways to authenticate are offered (e.g., signing in with Google/ Facebook vs. creating a new account), the system neutrally indicates the privacy implications of each option. I have already used this pattern and I can say that it is much better to let the user decide consciously whether they prefer to use a federated login, aware that certain profile data will be shared, or opt for separate credentials to keep the information segregated. Together, these security and incident management standards reduce the likelihood of privacy breaches and ensure a rapid response if they occur, while preserving user rights and security as much as possible.

To conclude this more extensive analysis of privacy standards, I present a table with practical examples of some of the most used standards in our day-to-day services that you have certainly already interacted with in an application or website.

Privacy Standard	Example Use Case
Location Granularity	Google Maps only shares the city rather than the exact location for traffic predictions.
Protection against Tracking	Mozilla Firefox blocks third-party cookies to prevent cross-site tracking.
Strip Invisible Metadata	WhatsApp removes metadata from uploaded images to avoid exposing

	location information.
Added-noise measurement obfuscation	Apple uses differential privacy to collect usage statistics without identifying users.
Onion Routing	Tor enables anonymous browsing by routing traffic through multiple encrypted #3s.
Anonymity Set	Anonymous search services like DuckDuckGo group users together to avoid individual tracking.
Use of dummies	A search app sends random queries to make it difficult to create user profiles.
Identity Federation Do Not Track Pattern	Apple Sign-in creates random emails for each service, preventing centralized tracking.
Pseudonymous Identity	Social networks like Reddit allow the creation of profiles without real identification.
Pseudonymous Messaging	Temporary emails help users communicate without revealing their identity.
Masquerade	Users can provide disposable telephone numbers when registering for online services.

Attribute Based Credentials	Age verification apps allow you to prove your age of majority without exposing your date of birth.
Obtaining Explicit Consent	Websites ask for explicit consent before storing non-essential cookies.
Lawful Consent	Newsletter forms require explicit opt-in to send promotional emails.
Selective Disclosure	LinkedIn users can choose to show or hide their connections to third parties.
Enable/Disable Functions	Google Maps lets you turn location history on or off at any time.
Selective access control	Facebook allows you to configure the visibility of posts individually.
Privacy Policy Display	Websites display privacy banners with a brief explanation of data use.
Dynamic Privacy Policy Display	Pop-ups inform you what data is being collected at the time of the interaction.
Privacy Labels	App Store displays badges indicating what data an app collects before installation.

Encryption with user-managed keys	ProtonMail allows you to encrypt emails without the company having access to the content.
Privacy dashboard	Google lets you view and manage activity history in a centralized dashboard.
Data Breach Notification Pattern	Companies notify users and regulators about data leaks within the legal deadline.
Unusual Activities	Banks block suspicious transactions and ask the user for additional authentication.

For mobile app developers on the most popular platforms, Apple and Google's privacy guidelines for app development follow stricter data protection principles, requiring developers to implement secure and transparent architectures. In the Apple ecosystem, apps must adhere to App Tracking Transparency (ATT), which requires explicit user consent before any tracking across apps and websites. Additionally, Apple requires applications to justify data collection in the Privacy Manifest and use secure frameworks such as Secure Enclave for storing cryptographic keys and Keychain for credentials. On Android, Google takes an approach based on data minimization and granular control, requiring apps to use Scoped Storage to isolate app data and reduce the need for invasive permissions, such as access to the advertising identifier (GAID), which now requires user consent.

From an architectural perspective, applications need to adopt sandbox security techniques to ensure the isolation of user data. On iOS, each application operates within an isolated container, with restrictive access policies defined by the App Sandbox, preventing external processes from accessing sensitive data. On Android, the use of FileProvider for secure file sharing between applications and the use of Auto Backup with encryption ensure that sensitive data is not unduly exposed. Additionally, both systems encourage the use of secure APIs to communicate with servers, recommending practices such as mandatory HTTPS with TLS 1.2+ and the use of restricted API keys to prevent credential leaks.

Developers must also pay attention to compliance with transparency rules when managing user data. On iOS, Apple requires apps to provide a Privacy Nutrition Label in the Appstore, detailing what types of data are collected and how they are used. On Android, Google Play requires the Data Safety Section, an equivalent that requires the disclosure of data collection and sharing practices. Additionally, both operating systems discourage the use of third-party SDKs that do not follow privacy guidelines and recommend implementing techniques such as Differential Privacy and secure local storage whenever possible to minimize exposure of sensitive data.

Does it seem like a lot? Every day new requirements, standards and responsibilities arise that make the life of a privacy engineer increasingly challenging.

Being up to date with and understanding these guidelines is a prerequisite for technical professionals who want to implement innovative solutions aligned with global privacy challenges. The scenario is dynamic, the demands are complex, but the impact of technical work on privacy is increasingly relevant and indispensable.

STRUCTURE OF A PRIVACY PROGRAM

As a technical professional, it is important that you know the type of project or journey you are part of. A privacy program is a structured initiative to ensure that an organization treats personal data ethically, securely and in compliance with global regulations and standards. It covers everything from the conception to the operation of systems, ensuring that data protection principles, such as minimization, transparency and user control, are applied at all phases of the data lifecycle, a topic we will see later.

The program involves the implementation of technical and organizational measures, such as the integration of privacy by design and by default, regular audits, and the use of specific tools for privacy impact assessment. This type of program not only mitigates legal and financial risks associated with privacy violations, but also promotes stakeholder trust and reinforces the organization's position in the market, especially in a scenario where privacy is increasingly valued as a competitive differentiator.

More practically, we can divide a privacy program into ten steps:

1. **Definition of program structure:** The professional must focus on understanding the strategic objectives of a privacy program, ensuring that it is aligned with organizational goals and not just legal requirements. This involves creating a solid foundation that incorporates privacy from the start.

2. **Privacy governance planning:** Work to establish an effective governance model that defines roles and responsibilities, including designating a DPO and integrating privacy teams with other functional areas. Clear documentation and communication about responsibility flows are extremely important elements.

3. **Identification of privacy requirements:** When gathering requirements, it is important to involve multidisciplinary teams to ensure that privacy needs are captured from the first phases of the systems development lifecycle. The focus should be on principles such as data minimization and transparency, as well as impact-based risk analysis.

4. **Integration into the software development lifecycle:** Embedding privacy controls directly into the SDLC is vital. This includes applying data security measures, conducting privacy impact assessments (DPIA), and designing solutions that prioritize data minimization and pseudonymization.

5. **Continuing education and training:** Privacy professionals should implement regular training programs to make technical and non-technical staff aware of data protection practices, covering topics such as security, risk mitigation, and AI ethics.

6. **Monitoring and auditing:** Implementing regular monitoring and auditing processes ensures that privacy policies are effectively enforced and allows for early identification of issues. This should include ongoing reviews of data collection and storage practices.

7. **Incident management:** Establishing a robust incident response plan is essential for dealing with data breaches. Preparation should include simulated exercises to ensure staff are ready to respond quickly and effectively to adverse events.

8. **Engagement with stakeholders:** The success of the privacy program depends on constant dialogue with all stakeholders, including end users, suppliers and regulators. Transparency in communications increases trust and makes it easier to adapt to regulatory changes.

9. **Technological adaptation:** Professionals must prioritize the adoption of emerging technologies that support advanced privacy practices, such as anonymization and encryption, and ensure that these solutions are scalable to meet future demands.

10. **Evolution and continuous improvement:** A privacy program is never complete; it must constantly evolve to keep up with changes in the regulatory environment, technological advances and user expectations. This requires regular reviews and adjustments based on metrics and feedback.

These steps were inspired by the IAPP recommended framework for a privacy program[17] (International Association of Privacy Professionals) but adapted for software engineering professionals.

As a technical professional, have you ever stopped to think about how you can contribute directly and strategically to the stages of a privacy program? From defining requirements to continuous evolution, your software and development skills are essential to embed more robust controls into the development lifecycle, ensure audits and monitoring are supported by tools, and help implement technical privacy measures. Can you see where your knowledge could be most valuable in each of these phases?

The software architecture team is very important in designing applications and infrastructures that incorporate privacy by design, adopting techniques such as data minimization, anonymization and granular access control. Developers implement these guidelines in the code, using practices such as end-to-end encryption, secure credential management and logging of sensitive activities with audit control. Their work is supported by security engineers, who establish frameworks for authentication, risk monitoring, and protection against data leaks.

The IT infrastructure and operations team actively collaborates to ensure data is stored and processed securely by adopting appropriate network segmentation, privilege management, and retention policies. This group works closely with database administrators, who implement techniques such as encryption at rest, data masking in test environments, and segregation of sensitive personal data. Additionally, DevOps professionals support with techniques to automate compliance with privacy policies, ensuring that each new software deployment passes rigorous security and privacy checks before being put into production.

The governance and compliance team acts as a point of convergence between all these areas, ensuring that regulatory and business guidelines are translated into viable technical requirements. These professionals collaborate with data engineers to ensure that big data pipelines respect consent rules and the purpose of information use. They also coordinate regular audits to assess compliance with privacy regulations, using continuous monitoring tools to identify potential compliance deviations. This interconnection between different roles within IT strengthens the company's ability to guarantee privacy as a fundamental pillar of its technological operation.

Lucas has always been a very skilled developer. At the startup where I worked, any piece of code I wrote needed to be efficient and secure. But until that Monday, he had never given much thought to data privacy. When he received notification that his company had been inspected for a privacy violation, he knew something was wrong.

The problem started months earlier when the company launched a new personalized recommendation feature. The algorithm, to be more precise, stored and crossed user information without considering whether that information was really necessary for the system to function. At first, no one saw a problem. After all, more data meant better recommendations. But now, a customer demanded the complete deletion of their data – and no one knew exactly where it was.

It was then that Carolina, the company's new DPO, took action. Her first move was to implement a privacy program, something Lucas had no idea what it meant until he saw her reorganize the entire company. First, it mapped all data flows, identifying where it was stored, how it was processed and who had access. Then, it defined clear rules: data would only be collected for a specific purpose and should be deleted when it was no longer necessary. The code would need to change.

Lucas spent the next few weeks refactoring the application. Introduced pseudonymization, encryption, and automatic retention rules. Each system request now passed through a "Privacy Gateway", ensuring that the principles of minimization and transparency were followed. When he finished the last line of code, he noticed something curious: the system was not only safer, but also more efficient.

Months later, the company underwent an audit and, for the first time, there were no irregularities. The privacy program was no longer just a set of policies – it was integrated into the very DNA of the software. Lucas, who at first thought it was just another piece of bureaucracy, now understood: well-done privacy doesn't hinder the product. On the contrary, it makes it something that users can trustr.

The structure of a privacy program shows how complex and important it is to ensure that personal data is treated ethically, securely and in accordance with regulations.

By covering everything from strategic definition to continuous evolution, the program not only protects the organization against legal and financial risks, but also strengthens stakeholder confidence and its competitive position. Through integrated practices, such as privacy by design, regular audits and training, the program establishes a cycle of continuous improvement, adapting to new regulatory and technological demands. Thus, a robust program is not just a legal obligation, but a strategic pillar that promotes sustainability and innovation in an environment where privacy is increasingly valued.

DATA LIFECYCLE ANALYSIS

The data life cycle in software development comprises the phases of creating, storing, using, sharing and discarding information. As a software engineer specializing in cybersecurity and privacy, I say that understanding these steps is the minimum you need to mitigate risks associated with processing data, whether personal or not. Why? Lack of adequate data flow planning can result in critical vulnerabilities, such as privacy exposures or security breaches. Therefore, always keep in mind the importance of integrating protection measures from the design phase to data deletion, aligning with global privacy regulations and also with good practices such as "privacy by design".

Let's learn a little more about these phases:

1. Creation

In the creation phase, data is generated or collected for the first time in the system. This can happen in a variety of ways, such as user-filled forms, IoT sensors, external system integrations, or activity logs. For a software engineer, this step requires careful design that minimizes data collection, ensuring that each entry point is secure and that data is collected with explicit consent when that is the most appropriate data processing hypothesis. Additionally, data input validation must be implemented to prevent the injection of malicious information or errors that could compromise the system.

2. Storage

Storage deals with where and how collected data will be kept. For a software engineer, this involves choosing appropriate databases or storage structures, ensuring that controls such as encryption, secure backups, and segregation between production, development, and test environments are implemented. Additionally, access policies should restrict who can query or modify the data. Also consider compliance with legal regulations, such as retention for specific periods, avoiding excessive storage of information. This largely depends on each regulation and sector, where there are often specific standards and time frames for data storage.

3. Use

In the usage stage, data is processed to achieve intended objectives, such as generating reports, offering personalized services or performing analysis. The software engineer must ensure that data is used exclusively for the purposes declared and approved by users, in accordance with regulations. Here comes the application of techniques such as pseudonymization or anonymization, if the data is used in analyzes or tests. Another point to consider is implementing audits to monitor data use and prevent abuse or unauthorized access.

4. Sharing

Sharing occurs when data is transmitted to third parties or made available between different internal systems. For software engineers, this requires the use of secure channels such as secured APIs, encrypted transport (TLS), and authentication with more modern and robust technology. Before sharing, it is important to assess the real need for transfer and ensure that the receiving parties comply with data protection standards. Clear policies about what can and cannot be shared help prevent inappropriate or excessive use of information.

In addition to data sharing guidelines, the international transfer of personal data is a critical aspect in the context of privacy. Data transfer between different jurisdictions requires attention to specific regulations that determine the assessment of adequate guarantees in the destination country. It is the controller's responsibility to ensure that transferred data is protected by safeguards such as standard contractual clauses or adequacy decisions by the responsible authority. In the event of failures or violations, both the controller and the operator may be held jointly and severally liable, especially when adequate technical and organizational measures are not implemented to protect the data during transfer. This joint responsibility reinforces the importance of partnerships with trusted operators who share a commitment to privacy, ensuring that cross-border data flows are treated with rigor and transparency to mitigate legal and operational risks.

5. Disposal

In the disposal phase, data that is no longer needed must be disposed of securely to prevent unwanted access or exposure. This includes deleting files from servers, wiping hard drives, and using proper techniques to erase data from backups. For the software engineer, this step involves implementing automatic mechanisms for removing data after the legal or contractual retention period has expired. It is also important to document disposal for audit and regulatory compliance purposes.

Each of these phases requires the software engineer to combine technical knowledge with attention to data protection regulations, ensuring that the data lifecycle is handled securely, efficiently and compliantly.

From a technical point of view, the software life cycle demands a balance between functionality and privacy. During systems development, it is common to face some challenges such as the integration of third-party libraries, which can access sensitive data even without malicious intent.

Sensitive data is personal information that, by its nature, may cause discrimination or damage to a person's privacy if it is improperly exposed or used. In the LGPD (Brazilian General Data Protection Law), this data includes information such as racial or ethnic origin, political opinions, religious convictions, genetic or biometric data, health, sex life or sexual orientation. In the GDPR (General Data Protection Regulation of the European Union), the definition is similar, covering information that reveals aspects such as ethnicity, religion, health, genetic and biometric data used to identify a person. In short, this is very personal information that requires reinforced protection to ensure that it is treated safely and respects the rights of each individual and thus avoids discrimination in the most varied forms.

For example, using APIs that do not adhere to data minimization principles may result in unnecessary exposure of user information. The application of methodologies such as "Privacy by Design" allows the incorporation of protection mechanisms in both the architecture and operation of the system, ensuring compliance with good privacy practices.

Risk management in the context of the data lifecycle involves identifying, assessing and mitigating potential threats. Among the main risks are breaches of confidentiality, unauthorized access and excessive data retention. The implementation of technical controls, such as pseudonymization and encryption, combined with regular audits will help you reduce these risks. Furthermore, carrying out Privacy Impact Analyzes (PIAs) allows you to anticipate and mitigate problems before deploying the system into production.

A practical example can be seen in the development of an e-commerce application. In this scenario, it is recommended to store only the data strictly necessary for order processing, discarding personal data that is considered sensitive after the transaction has been completed. In a project in the past, we implemented anonymization techniques for analytical reports, avoiding the exposure of personal data on management dashboards. These practices not only strengthened users' privacy but also reduced regulatory risk.

Information security in the data lifecycle must be a

priority to prevent leaks and improper access. The adoption of access controls, continuous monitoring of activities and regular team training are essential practices. Another notable incident I experienced involved the lack of segregation between development and production environments, allowing developers to access real data in test environments. After a forensic analysis, we implemented more sophisticated protocols, including separating environments and using synthetic data for testing.

ISO 27001 and ISO 27701 controls are fundamental in the life cycle of data in software, ensuring that each stage, from collection to deletion, follows security and privacy standards. At the time of data collection and creation, information classification controls ensure that data is labeled correctly, determining its level of sensitivity and protection requirements. ISO requires that personal and critical data be collected minimally, respecting principles of necessity and proportionality.

During storage and processing, ISO 27001 security controls dictate the use of encryption, data segregation and access management to prevent leaks and unauthorized access. Techniques such as encryption at rest and anonymization help reduce risks in systems that handle large volumes of data. Furthermore, ISO 27701, which complements 27001 with specific guidelines for privacy, establishes that systems implement traceability and auditing, ensuring that any activity involving data is monitored and documented.

In the data retention and disposal phase, ISO guidelines require systems to have defined policies for securely storing and irretrievably deleting information when it is no longer needed. This includes the adoption of techniques such as secure deletion in databases, overwriting disks and automated management of retention policies. The standard also recommends reviews at a certain frequency to ensure that stored data is not kept longer than necessary, reducing exposure risks throughout the entire data lifecycle where ISO controls help to establish a safe and efficient flow, minimizing risks and ensuring that the privacy and security of information is preserved.

Note that not everything we do aims to protect personal data, but rather to ensure an adequate level of information security and risk management, which, in the end, ends up increasing the maturity of the company and data protection ends up being a natural consequence when adding privacy concepts to already mature security projects.

Taking a complete data lifecycle approach goes beyond good practice; It is a technical and ethical responsibility to ensure trust, compliance and resilience in the digital ecosystem. The integration of security and privacy principles from the early stages of development is what is needed to build robust systems aligned with regulatory demands and user expectations.

CHECKLIST OF PRACTICAL ACTIONS

☐ I mapped the personal data processed in all company systems.

☐ I identified legal bases for processing personal data in the software.

☐ Documented data flows within the software lifecycle.

☐ Performed a risk analysis to identify possible vulnerabilities in the data.

☐ Established access controls for sensitive and personal data.

☐ I've enabled encryption to protect data at rest and in transit.

☐ Verified practices' compliance with applicable privacy regulations.

☐ Implemented activity logs that track data access and usage.

☐ Trained the IT team on data privacy and security.

☐ I developed a clear data retention and deletion policy.

☐ Created a response plan for incidents related to personal data.

☐ Periodically review the software lifecycle to improve privacy practices.

CHAPTER 2

Privacy Software Design

Incorporating privacy into software design goes beyond a technical requirement; it is a commitment to users and data protection regulations. This chapter explores how the principle of privacy by design can be integrated from the earliest stages of development, ensuring that systems are designed to minimize data collection, protect personal data, and enable clear controls for users.

PRIVACY BY DESIGN AND BY DEFAULT

The concept of Privacy by Design (PbD) is one of the fundamental pillars of modern data protection and was originally developed by Dr. Ann Cavoukian[18], former Information and Privacy Commissioner of Ontario, Canada, during the 90s. In a period when privacy was seen only as a complement or something to be implemented at the end of projects.

If privacy is only considered at the end of the project, there will be problems. Privacy by Design means designing systems that respect privacy before even the first line of code. Just as you don't build a house without planning where the doors and windows are, a well-designed system is already safe.

Dr. Cavoukian revolutionized this perspective by arguing that privacy should be integrated from the design of systems, products or services – and not treated as a last-minute concern. She presented PbD as a proactive and preventive approach that places privacy as a central element of the development lifecycle and not just as a regulatory requirement. Instead of correcting flaws and gaps in relation to privacy after a system is ready, Privacy by Design encourages that privacy be considered from the beginning of the project, permeating all its phases: from initial planning and architecture to implementation, testing and maintenance.

Privacy by Design is based on seven fundamental principles that guide its practical application - Let's analyze each one and how these principles would apply in practice for the software engineer:

1. Be proactive, not reactive, anticipating privacy problems and preventing them before they happen;

For a software engineer, this means identifying potential privacy flaws in the early stages of development. In practice, by defining requirements, you can conduct privacy impact assessments (PIA) to anticipate risks associated with data flows and implement safeguards before the system goes into production. For example, designing APIs that avoid unnecessary exposure of sensitive data is a practical way to be proactive.

2. Privacy as default setting (Privacy by Default), ensuring that personal data is protected even if the user does not take any additional action;

A developer can apply this principle by configuring systems to collect only strictly necessary data and ensuring that, by default, personal data is protected. This may include, for example, automatically setting restrictive levels of data sharing in an application, such as limiting who can access profile information on a social media platform.

3. Privacy incorporated into the design, ensuring that data protection is integrated into the core functionalities of the system or service, without compromising usability;

For software architects, this principle requires that privacy be an intrinsic functionality and not an optional feature. This can be implemented by choosing frameworks and technologies that support good data protection practices, such as encryption libraries and robust authentication systems, ensuring that systems are secure in nature.

4. Full functionality (Positive-Sum, not Zero-Sum), balancing privacy with other legitimate goals such as

security and performance;

Instead of compromising usability to meet privacy requirements, the engineer should look for solutions that offer both security and efficiency. For example, implementing homomorphic encryption can enable calculations on protected data, balancing privacy with advanced analytical features, without sacrificing performance.

5. End-to-End Data Protection[19]), ensuring that data is protected throughout its entire lifecycle;

A developer must ensure that data is protected at each stage of the lifecycle, from collection to disposal. In practice, this includes using TLS to protect data in transit, encryption for secure storage, and secure data deletion methods such as overwriting disks that contain important data.

6. Visibility and transparency, offering clarity on how data is collected, used and protected;

From an engineer's perspective, this principle translates into creating clear interfaces and accessible tools that explain to users how their data is being collected and used. An example would be the development of control panels to manage privacy permissions, intuitively showing what data is collected and why.

7. Respect for user privacy, placing the individual at the center of decisions and offering real control over their data.

For a developer, this involves designing systems that put data control in the hands of users. In practice, this can be done by implementing features such as one-click account deletion, granular consent options for different types of data, and clear notifications about the use of information, always ensuring that these decisions are respected.

As said by Dr Cavoukian for the IEEE magazine[20]

"...the task of privacy-aware systems engineers and architects

> *is to translate the Privacy by Design (PbD) conceptual framework into a set of specific and operationally viable tools. When applied by designers and project managers, these tools will ensure that business requirements, engineering specifications, development methodologies, security controls and best practices are developed or implemented in accordance with each project domain or scope – with privacy as the context."*

So, in practice, Privacy by Design is applied to projects in different ways. In a software development project, for example, it translates into practices such as data minimization (collecting only the data strictly necessary for the operation of the system), the anonymization or pseudonymization of personal data, and the implementation of encryption to protect data in transit and at rest.

In web and mobile applications, PbD can be seen in the development of transparent consent banners, which allow the user to manage their privacy preferences in a granular and intuitive way. Furthermore, the choice of secure architectures for data storage, such as cloud environments with end-to-end encryption, and the implementation of secure and auditable logs for monitoring access to information are clear examples of how PbD takes shape in a technical environment.

Another common example is creating user interfaces (UI) that intuitively incorporate privacy. A system that collects data for a registration form, for example, must offer an explicit opt-in option, stating clearly and objectively what data is being collected, why it is being used and with whom it will be shared. Furthermore, the design should allow the user to easily review, modify, or delete their data. With increasing concerns about privacy in digital environments, companies that adopt Privacy by Design not only ensure compliance with privacy regulations, but also gain a competitive advantage by transmitting trust and transparency to their users.

The application of Privacy by Design can be integrated into each phase of software development to ensure that privacy is a central pillar. When choosing technologies, opt for frameworks and libraries that support native encryption, such as using Flask with the Flask-Bcrypt extension to protect passwords from the start, rather than adding security as a later layer. In your system architecture, adopt the principle of data minimization by designing databases that collect only essential information — for example, using tables with pseudonymized fields (such as IDs instead of real names) and configuring automatic expiration of idle data with TTL (Time to Live) in MongoDB. Already in the user interface, implement granular consent controls, such as unchecked checkboxes by default for optional cookies on a React site, accompanied by clear explanations about data use, ensuring that Privacy by Default is intuitive and accessible to the end user.

Ultimately, Privacy by Design transcends the concept of simple regulatory compliance. It is a development philosophy that promotes the construction of products and services that are safer, more respectful and aligned with the fundamental rights of individuals. In a world where privacy is increasingly valued and regulated, incorporating PbD into projects is not only a smart choice, but a strategic necessity for any company that wants to innovate in an ethical and sustainable way.

Before we go into more detail about privacy by default, I would like to bring up a case of discussion with a client, already in more recent privacy eras, to show how privacy by design would apply in a unique way in a software development process.

When you're a systems engineer, an inevitable part of your job will be telling someone – be it a colleague, a boss or even a client – what they shouldn't do, no matter how insistent or enthusiastic they may be. The challenge is that these conversations often happen when someone believes they have had the idea of millions and only sees the positive side of innovation, ignoring risks or nuances.

Back in the early 2000s, when mobile devices began to become popular, the web scenario was very different. Web systems projects were often separate: there was a robust version for desktops and a "modest" and lighter version especially designed for cell phones and tablets. It was common to see subdomains such as "m.mobile.com" or even different addresses, such as "site.com/mobile", signaling to the browser that this was a more "humble" version of the website. And it was no wonder: cell phones at the time had limited capacity – they could barely support heavy images and videos were almost a mirage. The main concern was to deliver the basics, with simple interfaces, few resources and very low data consumption.

However, as the years went by, the tables turned. Navigation became primarily mobile. According to the StatCounter report[21], in 2023 more than 60% of global internet traffic already came from mobile devices. Modern smartphones have faster processing than many older PCs and can handle everything: 4K videos, complex graphics, and gigabytes of data. Those "mobile" projects stopped being a complement and became the priority. It was there that the concept of "mobile first" was born, which dominated software factories, digital agencies and IT departments.

However, while "mobile first" won the hearts of the entire market, other concerns began to emerge – including privacy. As a developer concerned about the topic, you start to hear phrases like "Privacy First? What nonsense." Because, for many, it still seems easier to fix it later than to plan for privacy from the beginning.

Once, an enthusiastic client came with a "genius" idea for an app. He wanted to use the user's geolocation to send automatic notifications on WhatsApp whenever the customer passed near a partner store. Apparently, something simple and straightforward: the store gains in sales, the customer gains in practicality, right? Wrong.

The idea was implemented without:

1. Request explicit permission from the user;
2. Assess legal and compliance risks;
3. Consider contextual consent: giving access to geolocation to view a shopping mall's store map does not mean that the user, freely and consciously, agrees to being bombarded with invasive promotional messages.

I tried to explain this to the customer. I presented examples of similar failures that had generated negative repercussions on the market – companies criticized, apps removed from online stores and image losses that were difficult to recover. I spoke about the concept of Privacy by Design and the importance of respecting users' fundamental rights. The answer? Something like: "But it's just a push! This is a small thing, nobody cares about it."

And here comes one of the most difficult roles for anyone who starts to worry about privacy: saying no.

Say no to projects that look incredible on paper, but that carry clear risks and negative consequences for both users and the business. In this client's case, I tried to show that launching a service without respect for privacy is a shot in the foot. Today, users have a clear expectation that their data will be respected.

Services that disrespect privacy soon became the target of public criticism, boycotts and, in some cases, very heavy fines.

In the end, the client didn't want to listen. I wanted to implement quickly to "take advantage of the holiday" and capitalize on store traffic. My decision was clear: I turned down the project. And it wasn't easy. As a developer, there is always the fear of losing a client or compromising an important contract. But as demands for privacy grow, a project like this could have severe consequences.

What I learned from this situation is that "Privacy First" is no longer optional. It is a standard that must be incorporated into any modern project, just as "Mobile First" was in the 2010s. Today, privacy is a priority – and it is up to us, technical professionals, to ensure that it is respected from the first line of code.

In the digital age, privacy is no longer just a legal requirement to become a central issue of personal security. With the growth in the use of connected devices and data collection, threats such as improper tracking and digital stalking highlight the real risks for users. Incorporating privacy from the first stages of software development, through the concept of Privacy by Design and security by design are important requirements to protect individuals and create trust in the systems we use daily.

Recent cases, such as Bluetooth tracking devices being used for malicious purposes, demonstrate the importance of implementing these practices. Companies like Google and Apple have already introduced solutions to notify users of potential improper tracking, showing how proactive design can prevent security incidents and improve the user experience. Developing systems with privacy as standard is not only a good technical practice, but also a competitive differentiator, allowing companies to stand out in a market increasingly sensitive to data protection.

The Case for Wireless Chips: When Bluetooth Hacks Wi-Fi

Have you ever thought that your cell phone's Bluetooth and Wi-Fi could be fighting each other — and worse, one stealing the other's secrets? A study[22] 2021, by Jiska Classen and other researchers, showed that wireless chips like those from Broadcom, Cypress and Silicon Labs (used in billions of devices) have a complicated flaw. These chips, which share antennas and spectrum to coexist without messing up the signal, end up becoming open doors for attacks. Bluetooth, for example, can tamper with Wi-Fi and even grab network passwords or manipulate traffic, all because of poorly protected coexistence interfaces. It's as if your neighbor used your key to enter your house without you noticing.

The problem lies in the way these chips talk to each other. They use direct signals, like wires or buses, to decide who transmits first — all to avoid collisions and maintain performance. It's just that these signs don't have decent security barriers. A Bluetooth chip can send commands to Wi-Fi and access things it shouldn't, like encryption keys or entire packets. To avoid this problem, one tip is to check if your devices' firmware is up to date — companies like Broadcom have already rushed to fill holes after this study. Another idea is to obtain an extra layer of protection in the software, such as isolating the permissions of each technology with something like sandboxing at the OS level.

The researchers tested this on real devices and managed to do things like using Bluetooth to inject fake traffic into Wi-Fi or steal credentials without anyone noticing. This happens because chips trust each other blindly, without true authentication. To avoid falling for this, it's worth simulating these attacks in your test environment — use a tool like Wireshark to see what's going on between the chips or even a Python script to send random commands and test the defenses. If you work with embedded hardware, take a look at the manufacturer's documentation: sometimes, there is a way to turn off these coexistence interfaces or limit what each chip can "say" to the other.

Ultimately, the study shows that security is not just code — it's hardware too. These "lateral escalation" attacks between chips are a warning to those who think that privacy is just a server thing. So let's be careful: always be suspicious of internal connections that seem harmless and test everything you can. If your project's Bluetooth is too friendly with Wi-Fi, it might be time to put a brake on this friendship before it becomes a big problem. After all, no one wants their cell phone radio to become a spy, right?

ARCHITECTURES FOR SENSITIVE DATA

Personal data refers to any information that allows you to identify, directly or indirectly, an individual, such as name, address, email or telephone number. This information is widely used by organizations and systems to provide services, personalize experiences, and meet users' needs.

On the other hand, certain categories of personal data are considered to be more sensitive and, therefore, receive additional protection in various regulations around the world. This information includes aspects such as racial or ethnic origin, political opinions, philosophical or religious beliefs, genetic data, biometric data (when used to uniquely identify a person), information about health, sex life, sexual orientation or affiliation with organizations, such as trade unions. Inadequate processing of this data can lead to significant risks, including discrimination or negative impacts on individuals' fundamental rights. For this reason, privacy legislation establishes more stringent requirements for its collection, processing and sharing, ensuring more robust safeguards to protect people's dignity and privacy.

An example of discrimination involving sensitive personal data occurred in the financial sector, where a credit granting algorithm inappropriately used data related to ethnic origin to determine loan eligibility. Although not an explicit criterion in the model, the indirect association of variables such as home address and employment history led to the disproportionate rejection of applications from individuals from minority communities. This practice generated financial exclusion and perpetuated social inequalities, highlighting the importance of regular audits and *fairness* to mitigate biases in systems that use sensitive data.

When designing systems to store and process personal and sensitive data, select a software architecture that prioritizes security and segregation. There are several architectures used on the market, among which the following stand out:

- **Monolithic**: All system components are integrated into a single application. Although simple to implement, it is unsuitable for dealing with sensitive data due to the lack of separation and difficulty in ensuring granular security.

- **Layered Architecture**: Divides the system into layers such as user interface, business logic and database. It offers better organization, but can still mix sensitive and non-sensitive data, creating risks.

- **Microservices Architecture**: System components are developed as independent services that communicate via APIs. This approach allows for greater flexibility and facilitates the segregation of sensitive data into isolated services.

- **Serverless Architecture**: Uses on-demand functions and managed services. Although it offers scalability, it requires detailed planning to avoid leaks or unauthorized access.

To protect sensitive data, effective segregation requires the use of robust techniques and consolidated frameworks. Some methods and practices include:

Creation of Separate Databases: Sensitive data can be stored in a dedicated database, isolated from the rest of the system. This reduces the attack surface and makes it easier to implement strict controls.

To implement database separations, the software will need to be tuned to identify, route and manage sensitive data independently from the rest of the system. A common technical approach is to use an abstraction layer or proxy to route requests for sensitive data to the appropriate database. This middle layer can be implemented using patterns like the Repository Pattern[23] or through a dedicated service, such as a Data Access Layer[24] (DAL), which dynamically decides which bank to send the query to based on the data type.

To support multiple databases, the software must be configured to allow simultaneous connections to different instances or clusters. This can be done by configuring multiple connection pools, where each pool manages connections to a specific database. Additionally, it is necessary to implement routing logic that determines the correct destination based on the context of the request. For example, an API can inspect the type of data requested and direct the query to the sensitive database or the generic database.

In terms of security, the dedicated database for sensitive data must be configured with restrictive access policies, use of encryption at rest (such as Transparent Data Encryption[25] - TDE) and end-to-end encryption in transport (TLS). Additionally, isolation can be strengthened by using private networks to limit access between different layers of the system.

If a proxy technique is adopted, tools like ProxySQL[26] or PgBouncer[27] (which work for MySQL and Postgres respectively) can be configured to automatically route queries to the correct database based on defined rules, such as table names or keywords in SQL queries. This avoids the need for direct adjustments to the application, but requires clear mapping and rigorous validation of routing rules to prevent sensitive data from being erroneously exposed in queries to the generic database.

With these practices, database separation is not only viable, but also scalable, offering greater security and flexibility to the system.

Data Encryption: Encryption, both at rest and in transit, ensures that sensitive data is unreadable without the proper key. Frameworks like AWS KMS[28] or Azure Key Vault[29] are often used to manage encryption keys, for example.

The software must be configured to apply encryption techniques both at rest and in transit, ensuring that sensitive data remains protected at every stage of its lifecycle. For data at rest, it is possible to use native encryption features offered by database management systems, such as Oracle TDE, transparent encryption in PostgreSQL, or alternatives configured in the storage itself. These solutions ensure that stored data is automatically encrypted, minimizing the risk of unauthorized access.

On Amazon/AWS, for example, you can enable this by default on RDS type databases[30].

For data in transit, it is worth setting up secure connections using protocols such as TLS. This can be done by adjusting the database connection parameters and application services so that all communication between parties is encrypted, preventing traffic interception.

Encryption key management is a critical component in this process. The software can be tuned to utilize trusted libraries that implement secure key creation, storage, and rotation practices, such as secure configuration managers or hardware security modules (HSMs) integrated into the infrastructure. The application must access the keys dynamically and securely, without exposing them directly in the code or in configurable files.

An additional approach involves the use of proxies or cryptographic intermediaries, which can perform encryption and decryption operations on data before its storage or retrieval. This intermediate layer simplifies software code, centralizes key management, and improves security by preventing keys from being directly accessible to the application.

With these implementations, sensitive data remains protected against unauthorized access, while the system remains efficient and compatible with good security practices and software architecture.

Tokenization: Replacing sensitive data with irreversible tokens allows the system to operate with less risk, as the real data is never directly manipulated. This technique is widely used in financial systems.

In this case, the software must be designed to replace sensitive data with irreversibly generated tokens, ensuring that the original data is stored and accessed only when absolutely necessary. In practice, this involves integrating a tokenization layer into the system, where data such as card numbers, IDs or other sensitive information is sent to a secure service that generates unique and irreversible tokens to replace the original data.

These tokens are stored and used in daily transactions by the system, while the actual data remains protected in a secure environment, such as a data vault or an isolated storage base, accessible only by highly restricted services. To manage this architecture, the software must include a mapping mechanism that allows you to convert tokens back to original data only when necessary, with strict authentication and access controls.

As an example, see how an algorithm made to tokenize a credit card number works in Python using the cryptography library.

```
from cryptography.fernet import Fernet
key = Fernet.generate_key()
cipher_suite = Fernet(key)
token = cipher_suite.encrypt(b"1234-5678-9876-5432")
```

```
print(token) # Output: b'gAAAAABl...'
```

The system can also be tuned to include tokenization proxies or gateways, which act as intermediaries to process tokenization requests and deter any direct access to sensitive data. These proxies help centralize tokenization logic, ensuring operations are consistent and secure.

Furthermore, to ensure high availability and scalability, the system must be prepared to manage a large volume of tokens and synchronize updates in distributed environments. This may include using token partitioning techniques or secure caching systems to improve performance without compromising security.

With tokenization, the risk of exposing sensitive data is drastically reduced, allowing the system to operate with greater security and reliability, especially in sectors where information protection is a critical requirement.

Role-Based Access Controls (RBAC): Implementing RBAC ensures that only authorized users or systems access sensitive data. Tools like Keycloak[31] can help manage authentication and authorization.

To implement role-based access controls (RBAC) effectively, software must be designed to identify and differentiate the permission levels of users or systems based on their specific roles. In practice, this involves clearly defining roles in the system, such as "administrator", "analyst", or "end user", and associating specific permissions with each of these roles. These permissions determine which resources and data can be accessed, as well as the operations that can be performed.

The application needs a robust control layer to check the permissions of each request before granting access to sensitive data or critical functionality. This can be achieved through the use of middleware that intercepts requests, validates authentication tokens and authorizes access based on defined roles. For example, authentication frameworks or libraries can be configured to issue JWT tokens[32] that include role information, allowing the system to authorize actions in a decentralized and efficient way.

Additionally, the application can integrate specialized identity and access management (IAM) solutions, which simplify the configuration and monitoring of RBAC in complex systems. Tools such as authentication proxies or dedicated services help centralize authentication and authorization logic, reducing the need to replicate these functionalities in the application code.

Finally, to ensure that RBAC is effective, the software must include auditing and monitoring mechanisms to record and review access attempts, identify potential violations, and adjust permissions as necessary. With these implementations, the system will be equipped to protect sensitive data, ensure compliance with organizational policies, and operate with greater security and efficiency.

In one of the biggest data protection scandals in the energy sector, Enel Energia was fined[33] in 79 million euros by Garante Privacy, the Italian data protection authority. The case revealed serious flaws in the company's security systems, allowing unauthorized agents to access its databases and use this information for illegal telemarketing practices. For years, customers have been targets of invasive phone calls, misleading promotions, and even contracts signed without actual consent. The fine, the largest ever applied by the agency to date, came after an investigation that discovered that Enel acquired 978 contracts from companies that were not even part of its official sales network.

The problem was not only the misuse of data, but also the lack of adequate controls in Enel's internal systems. Inspections revealed that the company's defenses were weak, allowing the entry of "procacciatori abusivi" — customer capturers who took advantage of vulnerabilities to operate illegally. In total, at least 9,300 contracts were activated through these questionable practices. This case highlights a critical risk for software engineering teams: the need to protect sensitive databases from unauthorized access. Measures such as strengthened authentication, suspicious activity monitoring and strict access restrictions are essential to prevent loopholes from being exploited for illicit business and to ensure compliance with data protection laws.

Physical and Logical Segregation: In more robust architectures, sensitive data can be stored on separate physical servers or in logically isolated clusters in the cloud.

To implement physical and logical segregation of sensitive data, software and infrastructure must be designed to completely isolate this data from the rest of the system. Physical segregation may involve the use of dedicated servers, where sensitive data is stored on separate hardware, with restricted physical access and specific security policies, such as network-level firewalls and VLAN segmentation. This approach minimizes the risk of unauthorized access and limits the attack surface to specific components.

On the other hand, logical segregation is widely used in cloud environments, where sensitive data is isolated in clusters or dedicated virtual instances. This configuration requires the use of separate identities, virtual private networks (VPNs), and strict access control policies to ensure that only authorized services or users can interact with these clusters. Infrastructure as Code (IaC) management tools like Terraform [34] or Ansible[35], can be used to define and apply these isolation settings in a consistent and automated manner.

When using Terraform to provision a secure VPC on AWS it is a simplified setup, for example:

```
resource "aws_vpc" "main" {
  cidr_block = "10.0.0.0/16"
```

```
enable_dns_support = true
tags = { Name = "vpc-segura" }
}
```

In the case of Ansible, you can integrate to harden the server:

```
- name: Desabilitar root login
  lineinfile:
    path: /etc/ssh/sshd_config
    regexp: '^PermitRootLogin'
    line: 'PermitRootLogin no'
```

And finally, configure GuardDuty for monitoring:

```
Ative via console ou CLI: aws guardduty create-detector --
enable."
```

With this pipeline you can increase the security of server configurations, for example. Don't forget that above I present just a few key excerpts in a more simplified way so you have an understanding of the possibilities, however, in the reality of your project you must understand how to incorporate each component in order to add more security and privacy.

In software, adjustments will be needed to ensure that applications know which servers or clusters contain sensitive data. This may include configuring connection proxies or middleware that routes requests according to the data type. For example, queries for common data can be directed to standard servers, while accesses to sensitive personal data are directed to segregated servers or clusters. This logic can also be integrated with authentication and authorization systems to strengthen control over who or what can access sensitive data.

By combining these techniques, physical and logical segregation not only increases security, but also facilitates compliance with organizational policies and reduces the impact of potential incidents, ensuring greater resilience and reliability for system operation.

In a case that raises serious concerns about data security in public hospitals, Centro Hospitalar Barreiro Montijo in Portugal was fined 400,000 euros by the National Data Protection Commission (CNPD). The offense involved serious failures to protect patients' medical information, resulting in indiscriminate access to sensitive data. The investigation revealed that the hospital did not have adequate controls to restrict access according to the needs of each professional, violating fundamental principles of data minimization and "need to know". The case came to light not through a formal complaint, but after a press report, showing that the flaws were publicly known even before any regulatory action.

The audit revealed an alarming scenario: 985 user accounts were associated with the "doctor" profile, but only 296 doctors were part of the hospital team. Furthermore, old credentials of professionals who no longer worked at the hospital were still active, and nine administrative employees had unrestricted access to clinical information. These vulnerabilities could have allowed any authorized user within the system to consult sensitive patient data without justification or adequate tracking. The hospital tried to defend itself by claiming that it used a system provided by the Portuguese Ministry of Health, but the CNPD rejected this justification, reinforcing that the institution itself was responsible for data security.

For software engineering and information security teams, this case serves as a warning about the risks of a lack of governance in access control. In environments where sensitive data is handled, such as medical information, implement rigorous user profile management, continuous access auditing and robust authentication.

Monitoring and Auditing: Use tools like Splunk[36] or ELK[37] to monitor access and activities around sensitive data, helping to detect anomalies or unauthorized access.

To implement effective monitoring and auditing, software and infrastructure must be configured to capture, store, and analyze detailed records of all activities related to sensitive data. This includes tracking unauthorized access, queries, modifications and access attempts. Tools like **Splunk**, **ELK Stack** (Elasticsearch, Logstash, and Kibana), or other log and event management platforms, can be integrated to collect and centralize this data, providing a comprehensive view of system operations.

In practice, the system needs to be tuned to generate detailed logs at each relevant layer, from the database to the application. These records must include information such as user identity, timestamp, type of action performed and the resource accessed. To ensure the integrity and security of logs, they must be stored in centralized locations and protected from unauthorized changes.

In addition to log collection, real-time monitoring must be configured to detect anomalous access patterns, such as repeated access attempts, higher-than-expected query volumes, or accesses at unusual times. This can be implemented with automatic rules-based alerts or with solutions that use machine learning to identify non-standard behavior.

The software should also include an audit layer, where administrators can view detailed reports and access histories. Customizable dashboards can be created using tools like Kibana or Splunk dashboards, enabling quick, actionable analysis of security incidents.

Finally, integration with notification systems such as emails or collaboration tools (Slack, Microsoft Teams) can help alert security teams in real time about suspicious activity. With these practices, monitoring and auditing not only increases visibility into the use of sensitive data, but also enables rapid response to potential threats, strengthening system security and compliance.

Data Masking: During development or testing, sensitive data may be replaced with dummy values that preserve the format but do not reveal real information. We have already covered some of these pseudonymization techniques previously.

To implement data masking effectively, software and development processes must be configured to replace sensitive data with dummy values, ensuring that real data is not exposed in test or development environments. Masking can be applied directly to databases or application layers, maintaining the format and structure of the original data so that systems and functionalities can be tested without compromising privacy.

In practice, specialized masking tools, or custom scripts, can be used to generate fictitious values. For example, in a column of credit card numbers, real data can be replaced with valid but fictitious numbers, preserving the format expected by the application. This can be done with masking libraries available in various programming languages or with enterprise data masking solutions.

The software must include logic to differentiate production and test environments, ensuring that real data is only accessible in production. During the process of extracting data into development or QA environments, masking scripts must be automatically applied, replacing personal data before the data is transferred.

For more complex systems, where multiple applications interact, it may be necessary to implement proxies or middleware that perform real-time masking, intercepting and replacing sensitive data before delivering it to test systems. Additionally, techniques such as temporary tokenization can be used to create surrogate data that behaves similarly to real data, but without any link to sensitive information.

With these practices, data masking allows developers and

testers to work safely in environments that reflect reality, but without the risk of exposing sensitive data, preserving system integrity and information security.

Segregating sensitive data using these techniques not only improves security, but also simplifies regulatory compliance and increases user trust. An approach based on multiple layers of protection creates a more resilient environment against attacks and leaks, ensuring that even if a part of the system is compromised, the most critical data remains protected.

This architectural model, when implemented correctly, promotes a balance between functionality and security, ensuring that systems meet data protection demands in the current scenario.

Pseudonymization, Anonymization and Data Minimization.

Anonymization refers to the process of irreversibly transforming personal data so that it can no longer be attributed to a specific person without the use of additional information that is separated. According to the most modern regulations, anonymized data is outside the scope of data protection legislation, as it is no longer personal data.

In other words, anonymized data is not personal data.

On the other hand, pseudonymization involves replacing direct identifiers with pseudonyms, maintaining an indirect link between the data and the individual through encryption keys or another secure mechanism. Unlike anonymization, pseudonymization also allows data to be re-identified under controlled conditions, meaning the data remains within the scope of data protection legislation.

In other words, pseudonymized data is still personal data.

Think of anonymization like tearing up a paper with information and scattering the pieces to the wind – impossible to reassemble. Pseudonymization is like putting a false label on a real name: with the right key, you can still find out who is who.

Data minimization is a central principle of privacy by design, requiring that only data necessary for a specific purpose be collected, stored, and processed. This prevents the accumulation of irrelevant information and reduces the risk of data breaches.

To begin implementing any technique like these, you first need to clearly delimit the purposes of processing, reevaluate the need for storing old data and, when necessary, use aggregation or anonymization techniques to reduce the granularity of the data.

ANONYMIZATION

There are several anonymization techniques and various software that can be used to apply these techniques, such as:

Generalization: Reduction in data detail (e.g., replacing a date of birth with an age range).

Generalization is a common approach in data anonymization. It works by reducing the level of detail of information. This can be done in several ways, depending on the type of data:

- Dates: Transform exact dates into ranges (such as 1990 to 1980-1990).
- Location: Use broader geographic levels (from "Street X" to "City Y" or "State Z").
- Numeric values: Group values into ranges, such as converting exact salaries to categories ($2,000 - $4,000).

This method is particularly useful when data needs to be shared with third parties, such as marketing analysts or researchers, without compromising the privacy of individuals.

Imagine that a fictional online store called TechStore carries out research to understand the demographic profile of its customers and optimize its marketing campaigns. During data collection, the team decides to include the customers' date of birth, as they want to analyze consumption patterns by age group.

Initially, the data collected includes information such as:

- Name: João da Silva
- Date of Birth: 03/15/1990
- City: São Paulo

When analyzing the risks, the team realizes that, by combining this data, it would be possible to re-identify individuals, especially in small cities or specific regions. To mitigate risk and preserve privacy, they decide to use the generalization technique.

The team applies the technique as follows:

1. Birth date generalization: Instead of storing the exact date (03/15/1990), they convert it to an age range: 30-40 years.
2. Location generalization: They change "São Paulo" to "Southeast Region".

After generalization, João Silva's data are represented as follows:

- Age range: 30-40 years
- Region: Southern Brazil

Thus, the TechStore team was able to protect their clients' personal data while still extracting valuable insights for their campaigns. This demonstrates that, with techniques such as generalization, it is possible to balance data analysis and privacy.

Disturbance: Introduction of statistical noise to mask sensitive data.

Perturbation is a technique that alters data by adding random noise. This is done to preserve privacy without losing statistical utility. Some common methods include:

- Numerical Noise Addition: Add or subtract random values, as in the example below.
- Data Swap: Replacing real data with similar values, such as rounding ages to multiples of five.
- Perturbation by Modeling: Apply statistical distributions, such as generating synthetic data with characteristics similar to the original set.

For example, imagine a startup called HealthPlus, which

develops health apps and collects user data to understand eating and exercise patterns. One of the data collected is the users' weight, used to create statistics on health trends in different regions.

However, the privacy team realizes that sharing this data directly, even if anonymized, may pose a risk of re-identification. They decide to apply the disruption technique to protect personal information.

A user named João enters his weight into the application: 72 kg. The perturbation technique adds a small "noise" to the original data. For example:

- A random number between -2 and +2 is added to the weight.
- In João's case, the random number generated is +1, so the stored weight becomes 73 kg.

The same technique is applied to all users of the database, resulting in a slight variation in the recorded values. Like this:

- Maria: From 58 kg to 59 kg
- Pedro: From 85 kg to 83 kg

The disruption technique has some similarity to the concept of "Differential Privacy" that we will see later.

Even with the weights perturbed, the mean and overall trend of the data remain roughly the same. For example:

- Original average: 72 kg
- Average with disturbance: 72.2 kg

With the perturbation technique, HealthPlus was able to protect user data while maintaining the ability to perform useful analytics for its public health campaigns.

Suppression: Removal of specific attributes. Tools like ARX are specialized and can be used to implement these techniques.

Suppression is an anonymization technique that consists of

completely removing certain attributes or information from the data set. Types of suppression include:

- Removal of Direct Identifiers: Deletes names, identification numbers, or exact addresses.
- Partial Suppression: Removes portions of information, such as showing only the first three digits of a zip code.
- Data Grouping: Replacing specific values with broader categories, such as converting "São Paulo" to "Southeast Region".

The company EducaData offers online teaching platforms and carries out research to understand the impact of its courses on different age groups and regions. The data collected includes name, age, city and performance on assessments. However, the privacy team detected that, in small towns, it may be possible to identify students based on a combination of information such as city and age. To avoid risks, they choose to apply the suppression technique.

A user called João again enters his information into the application:

- Name: João Silva
- Age: 17 years old
- City: Vila Pequena (population: 1,500 inhabitants)
- Final grade: 95

The team decides to remove (suppress) some data that increases the risk of identification, such as name and city, and groups age into a broader age range:

- Name: Removed
- Age: 15-20 years
- City: Southeast Region
- Final grade: 95

After applying the technique, the data from João and other students appears like this:

- Age range: 15-20 years
- Region: Southeast
- Final grade: 95

All information that could be used to directly identify an individual (such as name or exact location) has been suppressed.

With the suppression technique, EducaData was able to protect its students' data by removing information that could lead to identification. At the same time, the company maintained the ability to perform relevant analytics to improve the quality of its courses. This approach highlights how suppression is an effective solution for balancing data privacy and insights.

Each technique has specific benefits that make them more suitable for different scenarios. Generalization is optimal for broad categorical data, perturbation balances privacy and statistical precision well in numeric data, and suppression is the safest choice when absolute privacy is required. The choice of technique depends on privacy priorities and the need to preserve the usefulness of the data.

By way of comparing the benefits, I present a comparative table with the benefits of the three most common anonymization techniques.

Criterion	Generalization	Disturbance	Suppression
Reducing Re-Identification Risk	Limits details when grouping data (e.g., ages into ranges), making direct identification difficult.	It introduces noise into the data, making individual information less accurate without compromising analysis.	Completely removes identifiable information, eliminating any direct link to individuals.
Preservation of Statistical Utility	Maintains overall trends by reducing granularity, making it useful for pattern analysis.	Preserves aggregate statistics and trends by slightly changing individual values.	Useful for high-level analysis, but may miss important details depending on suppression.
Applicability	Ideal for scenarios where data needs to be grouped (e.g., age, location).	Recommended for quantitative or numeric data sets that require moderate protection.	Suitable for contexts where privacy has absolute priority over data details.
Implementation Complexity	Relatively simple; requires defining appropriate categories	Moderate; requires appropriate noise calculations and control	Simple, but may require adjustments to balance privacy and usability.

	or ranges.	over the impact on data.	
Impact on Privacy	Partially protects, but general information can still be used for re-identification with other combined data.	High protection, making re-identification difficult, but possible if noise is insufficient or predictable.	Very high protection by completely removing sensitive data.
Suitability for Large Databases	Highly suitable for large databases, especially for categorical data.	Good suitability, especially for large quantitative data.	Effective, but may reduce usefulness on highly detailed and diverse bases.

PSEUDONYMIZATION

Although ways to make it difficult to reverse and identify the individual, no pseudonymization technique can guarantee 100%, but it is possible to make it very difficult for a user with bad intentions.

Here I will bring 3 most common techniques, but you can apply a variation of them or even several techniques at the same time depending on the type of data.

Hashing: Transforming identifiers into cryptographic hashes.

Hashing is a technique that transforms data into a fixed sequence of characters (the hash) through mathematical functions. Key features include:

- Deterministic: The same input data always generates the same hash.
- Irreversible: It is not possible to deduce the original data from the hash.
- Sensitive to Changes: Small changes in the data result in completely different hashes.

Some common hashing algorithms include:

- SHA-256: Widely used for its security and speed.
- Bcrypt: Ideal for passwords, as it includes a "salt" to make attacks more difficult.

Fintech BankEasy develops a solution to securely store its customers' identification document numbers, used to authenticate financial transactions. Given the risk of critical data leakage, the security engineering team decides to apply hashing technique to protect document numbers.

João Silva is a BankEasy customer, and his identification number is 123.456.789-00.

The team applies a hashing algorithm, such as SHA-256, to transform the number into a unique and irreversible sequence:

- Original number: 123.456.789-00
- Hash generated: 29c3eea3f305d6b823f562ac4be35217a4af817e2a1c2ab0 6e1f4b7c0b8e723c

The system only stores the hash of João's number, never the real number. If an attacker accesses the database, they will only see something like:

- 29c3eea3f305d6b823f562ac4be35217a4af817e2a1c2ab0 6e1f4b7c0b8e723c

When João tries to carry out a transaction, the number provided is hashed again. The system compares the new hash with the stored one:

- Number provided: 123.456.789-00
- Hash generated: 29c3eea3f305d6b823f562ac4be35217a4af817e2a1c2ab0 6e1f4b7c0b8e723c
- As the hashes match, João's identity is confirmed.

By using hashing, BankEasy was able to protect its customers' identification numbers, drastically reducing the risks of exposure in the event of cyber attacks. The technique proved to be effective in balancing privacy and functionality, creating a secure system without compromising the customer experience.

Tokenization: Replacing sensitive data with non-reversible tokens without access to a secure mapping system.

Tokenization is a technique that replaces sensitive data with unique identifiers (tokens) that have no meaning outside a specific system. Key features include:

- Reversible under control: Tokens can be reverted to the original data only through a secure system that stores the mapping.
- No intrinsic meaning: Tokens contain no information derivable from the original data.
- Security by isolation: Sensitive data is stored separately from tokens, protected by additional layers of security.

Some common tools and frameworks for tokenization include:

- Vault (HashiCorp): Offers highly secure tokenization and key management.
- AWS CloudHSM: Enables tokenization combined with secure hardware modules.

Fintech BankEasy needs to protect its customers' credit card numbers used in financial transactions. To achieve this, it decides to implement the tokenization technique.

João Silva is a BankEasy customer, and his card number is 1234-5678-9876-5432.

When storing the card number in the system, it is replaced with a randomly generated token:

- Original card number: 1234-5678-9876-5432
- Token generated: tok_abc123xyz456

The actual card number is stored in a secure and isolated data vault, accessible only by authorized systems. The main database only stores the token:

When João makes a purchase, the token (tok_abc123xyz456) is sent to the payment system. This system securely retrieves the actual card number to complete the transaction.

In the event of a data leak, attackers would only have access to the tokens, which are useless outside of BankEasy's system.

Using tokenization, BankEasy has protected its customers' card numbers from leaks and unauthorized access. The technique has proven to be an efficient and secure solution, allowing financial transactions to be carried out reliably and in accordance with privacy regulations.

Cryptography: Encrypt data with robust keys. Frameworks like HashiCorp's Vault and JWT can facilitate pseudonymization on modern systems.

Encryption is a technique that transforms readable data into an encoded format that can only be decoded by someone who has the correct key. Key features include:

- Reversible: Allows you to recover the original data using the correct decryption key.
- Key-based: Encrypted data can only be accessed by authorized entities that hold the keys.
- High security: Makes data unreadable to third parties, even if it is intercepted.

Some common encryption algorithms include:

- AES (Advanced Encryption Standard): Widely used for its security and efficiency.
- RSA: Ideal for encrypting data that needs to be shared between different systems.
- Elliptic Curve Cryptography (ECC): Provides RSA-equivalent security with smaller keys, ideal for resource-constrained systems.

The e-commerce company ShopSecure needs to protect its customers' credit card data to prevent misuse in the event of attacks or leaks.

Maria Santos makes a purchase on ShopSecure and enters the following data:

- Credit card number: 4111-1111-1111-1111
- Name on card: Maria Santos

Before storing the data in the bank, the security team uses the AES-256 algorithm to encrypt it:

- Original card number: 4111-1111-1111-1111
- Encrypted data: 5f2c7d9aef9875b123ab...

The encrypted data is stored in the ShopSecure database. The encryption key is stored separately in a security module (HSM - Hardware Security Module), ensuring that only authorized systems can access it.

An HSM (Hardware Security Module) is a physical device designed to protect and manage cryptographic keys and perform critical cryptographic operations such as encryption, decryption, digital signature and key generation. It operates in an isolated and highly secure environment, preventing unauthorized access or manipulation, even in the event of intrusion attempts. Widely used in applications that require a high level of security, such as banks, payment providers and government systems, HSM ensures that cryptographic keys are not exposed outside the hardware, maintaining the integrity and confidentiality of protected data.

When Maria makes another purchase, the system uses the key stored in the HSM to securely decrypt the data and transmit the information to the payment gateway.

If the database is compromised, attackers will only have access to the encrypted data, which is useless without the corresponding key.

With the use of encryption, ShopSecure has ensured that its customers' data remains protected from unauthorized access, while maintaining functionality for payments and management. The technique proved to be a good solution for balancing security, privacy and usability in electronic commerce.

Each pseudonymization technique has unique benefits that make it better suited to different scenarios. Hashing is simple and ideal for validations, but it does not allow recovery of the original data. Tokenization balances security and functionality in systems that require secure internal processing. Encryption offers the most robust protection in situations that require confidentiality and the ability to recover data. The choice depends on the necessary balance between privacy, functionality and complexity.

See a comparative table of the benefits of the three techniques:

Criterion	Hashing	Tokenization	Cryptography
Reducing Re-Identification Risk	Replaces identifiers with irreversible hashes, making data inaccessible without access to the original.	Replaces sensitive data with tokens that have no value outside the system, protecting against re-identification.	Encodes data so that it can only be read with the corresponding key, protecting against leaks.
Preservation of Functionality	Good for verifications (for example, comparing hash values), but does not allow recovering the original data.	Preserves functionality by allowing internal operations without exposing actual data.	Allows full recovery of original data, useful in cases where it is necessary to restore customer data.
Applicability	Ideal for validation or authentication scenarios where data recovery is not necessary.	Suitable for systems that require secure data exchange between components or systems.	Used in contexts that require total confidentiality with the possibility of secure decryption.
Implementation Complexity	Simple; it only requires the application of a hash algorithm (e.g., SHA-256).	Moderate; requires implementing a secure mapping and token management system.	High; requires strict key management and advanced algorithms such as AES or RSA.
Impact on Privacy	High protection, as the original data cannot be recovered, but is vulnerable to brute force attacks.	High protection; Sensitive data is isolated and tokens are useless outside the system.	Robust protection against unauthorized access, as long as the keys are secure.
Suitability for Large Databases	Highly suitable for large volumes of data, with fast processing.	Good for moderate foundations; may require greater capacity for token management.	It works well, but can impact performance on very large bases due to crypto processing.

For developers, keeping pseudonymized data and re-identification keys in separate environments can help with your data segregation strategy. You can also implement detailed logs to track interactions with personal data and use static analysis tools to verify that data collection aligns with minimization principles.

DIFFERENTIAL PRIVACY

Differential privacy is a technique that adds controlled statistical noise to data or query results, ensuring that individual information cannot be inferred from the data set. The approach is designed to offer a balance between privacy and utility, enabling robust statistical analysis without exposing individual data. Its main features include:

- The results of an analysis are almost identical regardless of whether or not an individual's information is present in the data set.
- The technique is based on parameters that control the amount of noise, known as "epsilon", allowing you to adjust the balance between privacy and precision.
- It is widely used in systems that perform aggregate analysis, such as census data or health reports.

Tools like TensorFlow Privacy Differential[38] or Microsoft's DP engine are examples of practical implementations of the technique.

Differential privacy can be simply illustrated using the example of a coin being tossed, representing the introduction of random noise into data to protect individual information. Let's imagine the following scenario:

You are part of an anonymous survey where the question is: *"Have you ever consumed alcohol?"*. Naturally, answering this question directly may raise privacy concerns, especially in small groups.

Step 1: Flip a coin
Before answering the question, flip a coin honestly and observe the result.

- If it comes up "heads", answer "Yes", regardless of the truth.
- If it comes up "tails", go to the second step.

Step 2: Flip the coin again
Now flip the coin a second time:

- If it comes up "heads", answer "Yes".
- If it comes up "tails", answer "No".

What happens here is that the random noise introduced by the coin toss protects the privacy of your actual response. Even if someone sees your final answer, they cannot be sure if the answer is true because there is randomness built into the process.

- If you answer "Yes," no one knows whether this is because you actually consumed alcohol or because the coin result determined that answer.
- Similarly, a "No" answer also reveals nothing concrete.

When data from all participants is collected, researchers know that about half of the "Yes" and "No" responses come from the random noise introduced by the coin. They can adjust the results statistically to estimate how many people actually consumed alcohol, without having to directly expose individual data.

This simplified example demonstrates the central principle of differential privacy: protecting individual responses by introducing controlled randomness, while maintaining the usefulness of the dataset as a whole. In the case of large data sets, more sophisticated algorithms generate mathematical noise similar to the flip of a coin, ensuring that the aggregated information is useful but that the individual data remains protected.

Software engineers can apply differential privacy by incorporating controlled mathematical noise into the data or results of analyzes performed by their systems. This first requires a clear understanding of the data that needs to be protected and the desired level of privacy, measured by the epsilon parameter. This parameter determines the amount of noise that will be introduced, balancing individual protection with the accuracy of the results. For example, when dealing with aggregated information like averages or user counts, engineers can add controlled variances to make it impossible to identify specific information.

Practical implementation can be done using specialized libraries, such as the Google Differential Privacy Library[39], TensorFlow Privacy[40] and SmartNoise. These tools allow you to systematically and safely add noise, whether at the raw data level or directly in query results. During the development of machine learning models, for example, noise can be added to training gradients, protecting individual data without significantly compromising model accuracy. Similarly, in systems that produce public statistics, such as surveys or reports, differential noise can be incorporated directly into the calculated metrics.

Want to apply differential privacy? Use TensorFlow Privacy like this: set the noise_multiplier to 1.5 in a simple classification model. Test with a small dataset and see how the accuracy changes with more or less noise. It's a practical way to start.

The epsilon parameter (ε) controls the level of privacy: smaller values (e.g.: $\varepsilon = 0.1$) offer more protection, but can reduce accuracy. See a simplified example in Python:

```
from tensorflow_privacy import DPQuery

query = DPQuery.GaussianSumQuery(l2_norm_clip=1.0,
```

```
noise_multiplier=1.5)

# Add Gaussian noise to data
```

You can even test different values of *noise_multiplier* in your data to balance privacy without losing the usefulness of the data.

This process must be integrated into the software lifecycle from initial design through deployment and maintenance. Don't forget to adjust noise levels and perform rigorous testing to ensure data remains useful for aggregate analysis without exposing individuals. Engineers also need to continually monitor the effectiveness of the implemented differential privacy mechanism, adjusting parameters as necessary to meet privacy and utility requirements in different contexts.

ADVANCED PRIVACY PRESERVING TECHNIQUES

In this part, we will explore advanced techniques used to protect privacy in datasets. These approaches focus on ensuring that data is sufficiently generalized or altered to avoid individual identification, while preserving analytical value. Applying these techniques makes sense in scenarios where personal data needs to be shared or analyzed in compliance with privacy requirements.

This topic is a broad discipline and would deserve a work just on this subject, whereas I will stick to explaining some of the main points in a more objective way.

The evolution of data anonymization techniques has brought to the fore advanced concepts such as *k-anonymity*, *l-diversity* and *t-closeness*, which are important for protecting privacy in scenarios where large volumes of sensitive data are analyzed. These concepts emerged as a response to the growing challenges of anonymizing information in databases, especially in situations where simple anonymization standards, such as the removal of direct identifiers, proved insufficient to prevent the re-identification of individuals. The goal is to protect people's privacy and their personal data while maintaining the usefulness of the information for analysis.

These methods are widely used by organizations that handle personal data, such as hospitals, financial institutions, and government agencies. For these sectors, where the processing of sensitive data is inevitable, guaranteeing the anonymity of individuals is both a technical and ethical requirement, in addition to often being a legal obligation. For example, in scenarios of sharing data for scientific research or public policy making, you can ensure that personal information cannot be re-identified. Thus, professionals such as data engineers, data scientists and privacy experts are directly involved in the planning and application of these techniques.

The concept of *k-anonymity* states that each record in a dataset must be indistinguishable from at least $k-1$ other records with respect to a set of quasi-identifying attributes, such as age or gender. This model was initially designed to prevent simple re-identifications, but alone it does not solve problems of lack of diversity within equivalence groups, such as attacks based on homogeneous values of sensitive data. To mitigate these limitations, extensions such as *l-diversity*.

THE *l-diversity* advances beyond *k-anonymity* by requiring that the sensitive values within each equivalence group be sufficiently diverse. This means that even if an attacker can identify an individual's equivalence group, they will not be able to determine data or information related to the person with a high degree of confidence. However, this approach also faces criticism, especially in situations where the semantic relationship between sensitive values can be explored, leading to the development of the concept of *t-closeness*.

Finally, the *t-closeness* adds more stringency to privacy protection by requiring that the distribution of sensitive values within each equivalence group be "close" to the global distribution, according to a defined metric. This model is particularly relevant in scenarios where statistical analysis of data can expose patterns that compromise privacy. These three concepts form a robust foundation for data protection in a technical context, and are a central concern for organizations that want to balance individual privacy with the need to extract value from large data sets.

Explaining these concepts with mathematics is not the goal, so let's use real-world examples?

k-anonymity:

> Imagine that you are at a costume party with hundreds of people, all wearing masks and costumes identical to pirates. In this environment, it's impossible for anyone to pinpoint exactly who you are, because even if they know you're there, there are lots of other people dressed the same way. This is the principle of *k-anonymity*: ensuring that you are part of a group of people who are indistinguishable from each other, making it difficult for anyone to identify you based on available information.
>
> Now, think about an investigative reporter who wants to know who was at the party. He discovers that all participants left a record with three pieces of information: age, city and profession. Without the *k-anonymity*, it would be easy to cross-reference this information and identify you. But if the data were organized to ensure that at least k-1 people shared exactly these same characteristics, the reporter would have difficulty telling who is who, protecting their identity. It's as if the masquerade ball was repeated in the world of data, where your privacy is protected by a "disguise" shared with others.

l-diversity:

> Imagine a safe where several people's important secrets are kept, and each person is represented by a code that groups similar secrets, such as "likes sports" or "has a blue car". Now, let's say someone discovers your group's code, but within your group everyone shares exactly the same secret, like "you have a blue car." In this case, it is enough to know the group to deduce

everyone's secret. This is the problem that k-anonymity alone cannot solve, and that is where l-diversity comes in.

With l-diversity, the vault is reorganized to ensure that each group contains at least "ll" different secrets. So even if someone discovers your group, they still can't know what your specific secret is, because there are several possibilities. For example, in your group there may be people with secrets like "they like sports", "collect stamps" or "love dogs". Thus, even if the group knows, the exact identity of each secret remains protected. It's how to make sure the secrets are mixed and diverse enough to confuse any onlooker.

t-closeness:

Imagine you're in a room full of people discussing their musical tastes, and the groups are organized according to similar styles: rock, pop, or jazz. If each group were very small or had little diversity, someone listening to the conversation could easily guess individual tastes just by knowing which group you belong to. Even if there was some diversity, if a group's conversation was very different from the average of the entire room, it would draw attention and could reveal something about you. This is where the concept of *t-closeness*.

With *t-closeness*, group conversations are carefully organized so that the distribution of musical styles within each group is similar to that of the entire room. For example, if in the entire room 30% of people like rock, 40% pop and 30% jazz, each group would have a proportional mix of tastes. This ensures that even if you know someone's group, you can't infer much about their tastes because they look like the general diversity of the room. It's like making sure conversations aren't so different that someone can identify you just by listening from afar.

These techniques (*k-anonymity*, *l-diversity* and *t-closeness*) function as invisible layers of protection that make individual data more difficult to identify or exploit, maintaining privacy even when large volumes of data are analyzed. Ultimately, they create a balance between utility and protection, allowing valuable information to be used for research, public policy or product development, without compromising anyone's identity.

In the 1990s, the Massachusetts Health Insurance Group (GIC) decided to release hospital record data for research. This data was considered anonymous because direct personal information such as names and addresses had been removed. The idea was that without these details it would be impossible to identify the individuals behind the records. However, this assumption soon proved to be wrong.

A researcher named Latanya Sweeney, who at the time was a graduate student at the Massachusetts Institute of Technology (MIT), decided to investigate whether it was possible to re-identify people in this supposedly anonymous data. She knew that, even without names and addresses, other information, such as date of birth and gender, could be used to cross-reference data with other public sources. That's exactly what she did.

Sweeney gained access to a public database of voters in the city of Cambridge, which contained information such as name, address, date of birth and gender. Using this information, she cross-referenced the data with anonymous hospital records. To his surprise, he managed to identify several people, including the governor of Massachusetts at the time, William Weld.

Governor Weld's case became emblematic. Sweeney discovered that with just three basic pieces of information: Zip code, date of birth and gender, it was possible to identify a specific person in an anonymized data set. In Weld's case, she was even able to send him a copy of her own hospital record, showing how his privacy had been compromised.

This case was a wake-up call for the privacy and data protection community. It showed that simple anonymization, which only removes names and addresses, is not enough to protect people's identities. When combined with other datasets, even seemingly harmless information can be used to re-identify individuals.

Sweeney's work has had a significant impact on the way data protection is handled. It has led to the development of more advanced data protection techniques, such as k-anonymity, which ensure that each record in a dataset cannot be distinguished from a certain number of other records. Additionally, the case helped shape modern regulations, such as GDPR in Europe, that require stricter measures to protect privacy.

Today, Governor Weld's case is often cited as a classic example of the risks of data re-identification. It serves as a reminder that in an increasingly connected and data-rich world, privacy is a complex challenge that requires robust solutions and continued attention.

Another real-world example is the anonymization of data in healthcare systems. Imagine hospitals sharing medical records to analyze disease patterns and improve treatments. If this data is released without protection, a person could be identified based on characteristics such as age, city and health condition. That's where these concepts come in: *k-anonymity* ensures that each patient is "mixed" with at least k–1 others with similar characteristics; *l-diversity* ensures that diagnoses or treatments within each group are diverse enough to avoid direct deductions; and *t-closeness* makes data from each group reflect general trends, without exposing sensitive differences that could lead to re-identification. Without us realizing it, these techniques make it possible for health policies to be created or scientific studies to advance without sacrificing our privacy.

See how interesting the case known as "How To Break Anonymity of the Netflix Prize Dataset" is[41] It was a demonstration of how it is possible to re-identify individuals even in datasets considered "anonymized". The study showed that by combining the Netflix Prize dataset, which included supposedly anonymously provided film rating information, with publicly available data on IMDb, it was possible to re-identify specific users.

The researchers revealed that around 80% of users who rated just 6 films in the Netflix dataset could be re-identified if the review information includedm approximate dates and were compared with another public set, such as IMDb. This methodology, known as *linkage attack*, explores overlaps between different datasets, associating records that share similar characteristics, such as review dates or specific film preferencesis.

This case highlighted vulnerabilities in the practice of data anonymization, highlighting that traditional methods, such as simply removing direct identifiers (name, email, etc.), are not sufficient to protect privacy. The implications of this study were profound, sparking debate about the effectiveness of anonymization and encouraging the use of more robust techniques, such as differential privacy.

The article "SoK: Managing Risk of Binding Attacks on Data Privacy"[42] describes strategies to mitigate the risks of linkage attacks, which occur when anonymous data is re-identified through correlation with other publicly available datasets, as was the case in the Netflix example. These attacks pose a significant threat to privacy, even when data appears to be anonymized. To address this, the article highlights several practices and technical approaches that can be adopted to reduce vulnerability.

The authors suggest the application of advanced anonymization techniques, such as k-anonymity, l-diversity and t-closeness and emphasize the importance of integrating differential privacy techniques, which introduce controlled noise into the data to limit the precision of possible inferences without compromising their general usefulness.

Another suggested approach is limiting the collection and sharing of personal data based on data minimization principles. This includes restricting collection to the minimum necessary to achieve stated objectives, storing data in a distributed manner to reduce the likelihood of direct correlations, and regularly monitoring re-identification risks using continuous audits and automated tools to detect potential vulnerabilities in anonymized data and strengthen security in dynamic data use environments.

DATA MINIMIZATION TECHNIQUES

Data minimization is a fundamental principle in data protection and privacy. It is based on collecting, using and storing only the minimum amount of personal information necessary to achieve the specific purposes of processing. This chapter will cover the main techniques, benefits and challenges of implementing this concept in the software development life cycle.

In a busy city where people were increasingly concerned about protecting their personal data, a small startup called DataGlow was starting to stand out. Founded by Clara, a software engineer passionate about privacy, the company's mission was to create technological solutions that balanced functionality and data protection.

Clara received a contract to develop a medical appointment scheduling app. The client's requirements seemed simple: allow patients to book appointments, choose specialists, and receive reminders. However, when reviewing the briefing, Clara realized that the client had requested the collection of personal data, such as identification document, full address and detailed medical history, even for basic functionalities. That raised an alert!

During an initial meeting with the client, Clara proposed a different approach. "Why do we need all this information at the initial registration?" she asked. The client, a little surprised, explained that he thought this data could be useful in the future, perhaps for marketing campaigns or internal reports. Clara calmly explained the risks of this approach and suggested that they apply the data minimization methodology.

She began tweaking the system design, questioning every piece of data requested. For the initial registration, basic information was restricted: name, email and telephone number, the minimum necessary to schedule an appointment and send notifications. Medical histories, although useful to specialists, would be provided by the patient only at the time of consultation, and directly to the doctor, without unnecessary storage in the system.

While implementing the solution, Clara also designed the system to use pseudonymization, ensuring that even in the event of a breach, personal data and sensitive personal data could not be directly linked to individuals. Additionally, it integrated transparent notices into the app, informing users about how their data would be used. For Clara, this was not just a technical obligation; it was a matter of respect.

When the app was launched, it received praise from patients and healthcare professionals alike. Users felt more confident knowing their data was being collected sparingly, while the client realized that Clara's approach not only increased trust but also simplified compliance with privacy regulations. Clara, looking at the positive impact of her solution, knew that she had transformed a technical project into an opportunity to drive a cultural change in how data is handled.

Thus, DataGlow not only delivered a successful product, but helped shape a new way of thinking about technology, where data minimization was not seen as an obstacle, but as an opportunity to build trust and security in an increasingly digital world.

The practice of data minimization starts at the design stage. At this stage, software engineers must perform analysis to identify which data is strictly necessary and how it will be processed. The use of frameworks such as LINDDUN or Privacy by Design strategies helps to identify and reduce excess collection. For example, when developing a user registration system, it is often enough to request name and email, instead of personal data such as identity number or date of birth. This approach not only protects individuals but also reduces the attack surface of potential data breaches.

By the way, LINDDUN[43] is a methodology designed for analyzing privacy threats in the context of software systems. Its objective is to help developers, software engineers and privacy experts identify, evaluate and mitigate threats that may compromise users' privacy. The name LINDDUN is an acronym that represents different types of privacy threats:

1. **Linkability (Traceability)**: The ability to connect a user's data or actions, even if anonymized.
2. **Identifiability (Identificabilidade)**: The possibility of identifying an individual from processed information.
3. **Non-repudiation**: The inability of an individual to deny actions or transactions carried out.
4. **Detectability (Detectabilidade)**: The possibility of determining whether specific data is present in a system.
5. **Disclosure of Information**: The exposure of private information to unauthorized parties.
6. **Unawareness**: The user's lack of clarity or understanding about how their data is used.
7. **Non-compliance**: Failure to comply with privacy regulations or user expectations.

This approach offers a systematic and detailed view of privacy, providing a solid foundation for developing systems that respect users' privacy and minimize risks associated with the collection and processing of personal data.

Another important technique is the use of anonymization and pseudonymization, powerful tools to guarantee privacy while still allowing the use of data for analysis or machine learning, as per the previous chapter. Anonymization eliminates the possibility of identifying an individual in data, while pseudonymization replaces direct identifiers with artificial codes, allowing re-identification only under controlled conditions. Despite this, such practices must be constantly reviewed, given that technological advances can compromise previously secure methods, as revealed by studies on re-identification risks.

One of the most common situations I faced was changing existing systems with a large legacy base where it would be necessary to apply data minimization techniques. See this other case:

Imagine an e-commerce platform called ShopSmart, which has been operating for more than a decade. Over the years, the company has accumulated a vast database, including information from customers who no longer use the service, duplicate data, and even over-collected personal data. The company's leadership decided to review its data management practices to adhere to privacy regulations, improve security, and reduce privacy risks.

The responsible software engineer, Rafael, started the process with a complete audit of the system. He and his team analyzed the database to map all types of stored information, identifying obsolete, redundant and excessive data. For example, they found customer records that had been inactive for more than five years, activity logs that no longer had a practical purpose, and critical information such as ID numbers collected during old campaigns.

Rafael created an action plan divided into stages. First, it implemented a process of "skeletonizing" legacy data. To do this, it used techniques such as anonymization and aggregation. Data that was no longer needed was anonymized or removed, preserving only what was mandatory for historical analysis, such as aggregate sales trends.

It then developed retention policies based on the data lifecycle. Inactive customer data was scheduled for deletion after a predetermined period, unless there was a legal justification for retention. This policy was automated to reduce human error and ensure new data followed the same rules.

In parallel, Rafael integrated additional layers of pseudonymization into the active system. Identifiable information such as emails and telephone numbers were protected with alternative identifiers, accessible only by systems that required this level of detail, such as customer support staff.

Finally, Rafael worked on a transparent interface that communicated to users how their data was being processed and allowed manual deletion of information on demand, in accordance with data deletion or review requests made by data subjects.

The result was a leaner, safer system aligned with best data protection practices. In addition to reducing the risks of leaks and regulatory fines, Rafael demonstrated that it is possible to apply the concept of data minimization to legacy systems, transforming a technical challenge into a competitive differentiator for ShopSmart.

The projects led by Rafael and Clara have one thing in common: they both face the challenge of aligning technological systems with data minimization practices, promoting efficient and secure management of personal information. Although the contexts are different, with Clara dealing with the design of a new system and Rafael working on a robust legacy, both projects require a strategic approach that balances functional needs with the responsibility to protect users' privacy. This similarity demonstrates that regardless of the stage of development, applying minimization principles is a critical step to building trust, reducing risk, and ensuring regulatory compliance.

In the following table, it is possible to observe how the actions taken by Rafael and Clara connect around common objectives, despite their specific differences in context. This comparison allows us to better understand the practical challenges and possible solutions in different scenarios. Additionally, the included checklist offers a practical guide for professionals who wish to replicate or adapt these practices in their own projects. Use these tools as a reference to structure your work and ensure it aligns with the highest data security and privacy standards.

Aspect	Clara's Challenges (New System)	Rafael's Challenges (Legacy System)	Action Checklist
Identification of required data	Determine the minimum required for basic functionality.	Map and categorize data accumulated over years.	Map and validate necessary data.
Processing of sensitive data	Avoid excessive collection in initial system design.	Identify unnecessary sensitive data in legacy.	Implement controls for collection and use of sensitive data.
Implementation of anonymization/ pseudonymization	Incorporate anonymization from the beginning of development.	Analyze and implement anonymization on old data.	Use tools for anonymization/ pseudonymization.
Defining retention policies	Plan data retention already in the system design.	Create retention policies for existing data.	Define and automate clear retention policies.
Transparent communication with users	Educate users about data usage and purpose from the beginning.	Ensure that users understand and accept changes.	Create clear and accessible communication for users.
Compliance with regulations	Ensure the system is built with native compliance.	Adapt the legacy system to current regulations.	Perform audits to ensure regulatory compliance.
Process automation	Automate collection and processing from launch.	Automate the deletion and retention of legacy data.	Integrate automation for continuous processes.
Reduction of operational risks	Mitigate risks of overspecification in the new system.	Reduce disruption risks when changing existing systems.	Monitor and review impacts on critical functionalities.
Engagement with stakeholders	Convince the customer to prioritize data minimization.	Get internal support for complex data changes.	Involve stakeholders in discussions and key decisions.

The challenge of data minimization lies in the need to balance system functionality and regulatory requirements. Organizations face dilemmas, especially in large-scale projects or in sectors such as healthcare and finance, where data is critical. The implementation of robust minimization strategies must be supported by ongoing developer training and regular process audits. The adoption of mechanisms such as granular access controls and activity logs can mitigate risks, increasing user and stakeholder trust in the system.

COOKIE MANAGEMENT FOR PRIVACY

Cookies are small sets of data stored in a user's browser when they access a website. These files contain information that allows the website to "remember" your interactions and preferences, such as language chosen, items added to the shopping cart or pages previously visited. Although they are widely used to improve the user experience, cookies also serve to collect data for content personalization, performance analysis and targeted advertising.

Once upon a time there was a young girl called Marina, who loved plants. One sunny Saturday, she decided it was time to turn her apartment into a jungle. With that in mind, he accessed a website called "Dream Gardens", which promised to transform any space into a botanical paradise. Marina spent hours browsing the website, adding exotic plants to her cart, but in the end she decided it would be better to wait for next month, when her salary arrived.

The next day, he started to notice something strange. As she scrolled through her social media feed, there was an ad for "Dream Gardens", displaying exactly the ferns and orchids she had added to her cart. "Coincidence", thought Marina. But the coincidence continued. While watching a recipe video on YouTube, a banner popped up on the screen: "Turn your home into a jungle! Buy our plants now!" Even in the weather forecast app, where Marina was looking for information about rain, a popup said: "Your plants dream of you. Get them today!"

Marina started to get suspicious. Each click seemed to lead to more ads. She no longer knew if she really wanted this or if it was the algorithm that wanted to convince her of this. Trying to escape, he decided to go for a walk, away from screens. In the middle of the walk, a notification on her cell phone interrupted her: "You forgot your stroller! Don't leave your plants waiting."

Tired of being persecuted for the plants she didn't buy, Marina decided to take action. He researched cookies and tracking online and discovered that the site had collected browsing data and shared it with advertising networks. Determined to change the game, she installed ad blockers and began refusing unnecessary cookies on every website she visited. The next day, when he opened his browser, he felt free. No banners, no pop ups, no green digital monsters chasing.

Marina never looked at cookies the same way again. What about plants? She bought some at a local store and discovered that the jungle of her dreams didn't need algorithms, just some dirt, sun and a lot of patience.

Cookies are considered personal data because they can identify or make an individual identifiable. Even though, on its own, a cookie does not contain information such as name or address, it can be combined with other collected data, such as IP addresses or browsing histories, to create detailed user profiles. This ability to link information and create unique identifiers is what makes cookies subject to more common privacy regulations.

In 2019, a telecommunications company was fined by the French Data Protection Authority (CNIL) for storing cookies on users' devices without valid consent. The case generated wide repercussions, as cookies allow tracking of online activity for advertising purposes without users being properly informed or having the option to reject tracking. This episode highlighted the risks of neglecting transparency practices and responsible use of cookies, reinforcing the need for regulatory compliance.

According to ePrivacy guidelines, cookies are treated as data collection tools that require user consent before being activated, except when strictly necessary for the website to function. Regulations establish that users must be clearly informed about what types of cookies are being used, their purposes and the possibility of managing their preferences. The aim is to ensure transparency and control, allowing users to make informed choices about the collection and use of their data.

Cookies can be classified into several categories, including strictly necessary, performance, functionality and advertising cookies. Strictly necessary cookies are essential for the website to function properly, such as those that keep the user logged in active. Performance ones help measure the effectiveness of the website, while functionality ones store user preferences, such as language or layout. Advertising cookies track user behavior across different websites to display personalized advertisements.

Each website must treat cookies according to their category, respecting regulatory requirements and user expectations. Strictly necessary cookies can be activated without prior consent, but must still be disclosed in the privacy policy. On the other hand, performance, functionality and advertising cookies require the user's explicit consent before they are activated. Furthermore, the website must offer accessible mechanisms so that users can review and change their preferences at any time, ensuring a transparent digital experience that complies with data protection laws.

For developers who want to ensure proper handling of cookies on their websites, a key practice is to implement a consent banner that complies with regulations. This banner must be displayed before any non-mandatory cookie is activated, offering the user clear information about the cookie categories and their purposes. Furthermore, consent must be granular, allowing visitors to accept or reject cookies on an individual basis, such as those for advertising, analytics or functionality.

Another technical recommendation is to adopt the concept of "lazy loading" for cookies. This means that non-essential cookies, such as tracking and analysis cookies, should only be activated after the user has given their consent. It is also important to store these consents securely, with records that can be audited, if necessary. Furthermore, programmers should use techniques such as hashing to anonymize identifiers in cookies, protecting personal information and minimizing risks of exposure. Periodic reviews of cookie code and policy are also essential to ensure that new features or integrated services are in line with evolving regulations.

The "Planet49" case[44] was a significant ruling by the Court of Justice of the European Union (CJEU) involving the practice of cookie consent on websites. In this case, Planet49, a German company, used a pre-selected consent method in an online promotion, where users were required to accept cookies as a condition of participating in a prize draw. The case raised critical questions about what constitutes valid consent under European data protection laws, specifically the General Data Protection Regulation (GDPR) and the ePrivacy Directive.

The CJEU ruled that pre-screened consent is not valid. The court concluded that, to be considered legitimate, consent must be informed, explicit and active. This means that users should have the option to consciously decide about the use of cookies, without the default settings already implying acceptance. Furthermore, the decision highlighted the need to provide clear and understandable information about the types of cookies used and their purpose, ensuring that users can make informed choices.

This case highlighted the importance of transparency and technical compliance in relation to the use of cookies. It also served as a warning to companies that use similar practices, highlighting the need to review their approaches and implement measures that respect users' rights. The CJEU's ruling reaffirmed the obligation to obtain explicit consent, protecting users' data privacy and setting a significant precedent for online privacy practices.

To check whether a website is respecting users' privacy regarding the use of cookies, you can use the browser's native tools or specific extensions.

One way to do this is by going to the website you want to analyze and opening the browser's development tools. To do this, press F12 or Ctrl + Shift + I (Windows/Linux) and Cmd + Option + I (Mac), or right-click on the page and select "Inspect". In the panel that will open, look for the "Application" tab (or "Application", depending on the browser language). Within this tab, locate the Storage section and select "Cookies". From there, a list of domains related to the site will be displayed; click on the main domain to view the stored cookies.

If you prefer a more accessible alternative, you can install extensions aimed at analyzing cookies and trackers, such as "EditThisCookie", "Cookie-Editor" or "Ghostery", which provide a simplified and detailed view of the cookies in use, making it easier to verify compliance with privacy practices.

Check whether the website has created non-essential cookies before you have given explicit consent. Non-essential cookies are often associated with tracking, analytics or advertising, and may include tool names such as Google Analytics or Facebook Pixel. Review information columns such as "Name," "Domain," "Expires," and "Value." If you identify cookies that do not fall into the strictly necessary category for the website to function shortly after initial loading, it is likely that your website is not compliant.

The Case for Third-Party Cookies: When Publishers Pay the Price

Think about a scenario where publishers, those sites that live off ads, start to realize that third-party cookies are costing too much — not just in money, but in terms of privacy as well. An article[45] of 2024 Digiday showed how companies like The Washington Post and Axel Springer are tired of the data leaks these cookies cause. They deliver valuable information, like what you read or buy, straight to ad networks, often without control. A Deloitte study cited in the text found that publishers lose up to 50% of their revenue because of these leaks, while users are exposed to rampant tracking. This makes it clear that poorly planned security can cost more than it seems.

The problem lies in the way these cookies work: they are released on the internet by third parties, such as advertising platforms, and collect data without the original website being able to hold the reins. This opens up gaps for leaks, as the publisher doesn't always know where the information is going. A simple solution is to cut these cookies from the beginning. You can set your website to only use first-party cookies, which are under your control. On the backend, you can adjust the server — like Nginx — to block third-party scripts by default, using headers such as Content Security Policy (CSP). This way, you decide who sees user data, not just any company.

The Washington Post, for example, began testing alternatives such as Seller Defined Audiences (SDA), which lets publishers manage data without depending on third parties. This reduces the risk of leaks and still keeps your ads running. As a developer, you can implement something similar: store behavior data on a secure local server and only share anonymous hashes with partners, like SHA-256 of user IDs. Another idea is to test tools like Google's Privacy Sandbox, which replaces third-party cookies with more controlled APIs. The secret is to always check the data flow — use a debugger like Chrome's to see what is being sent and to whom.

Publishers are waking up to the fact that security is not just a technical issue, but a way to protect users' wallets and trust. Axel Springer has already cut ties with cookies that do not add direct value, focusing on first-party data. For you, the lesson is clear: invest in solutions that give you control, such as basic encryption in first-party cookies or strict consent policies in the frontend. Cases like this prove that letting go of poorly managed third parties is not just fashionable — it is a necessity for those who want to maintain privacy and profit in the game.

DATA SUBJECT SUPPORT

DSAR (Data Subject Access Request) is a mechanism that allows data subjects to request access to the information that an organization holds about them. This process, provided for in most privacy regulations, is one of the pillars of the right to privacy, allowing individuals to exercise greater control over their personal data. The DSAR may include requests to access, correct, delete or restrict the processing of information, among others, thus ensuring informational self-determination.

Informational self-determination is the principle according to which individuals have the right to control the personal data that concerns them, deciding how this information is collected, used, stored and shared. This concept summarizes the idea that personal data belongs to individuals, not to the organizations that process it, ensuring that each person can determine the fate of their information in a free, conscious and informed way.

In the words of Danilo Doneda[46]:

> *Informational self-determination basically emerged as an extension of the freedoms present in second generation laws, and there are several specific changes in this sense that can be identified in the structure of these new laws. The processing of personal data was seen as a process, which did not end with the simple permission or refusal of the person to use their personal data, but sought to include them in successive phases of the process of processing and use of their own information by third parties, in addition to including some guarantees, such as the*

duty to provide information.

Informational self-determination was, however, the privilege of a minority who decided to face the economic and social costs of exercising these prerogatives. Once this exclusivist nature was verified, a fourth generation of data protection laws, like those that exist today in several countries, emerged and was characterized by seeking to overcome the disadvantages of the individual approach that existed until then. These laws seek to focus on the integral problem of information, as they assume that the protection of personal data cannot simply be based on individual choice – instruments are needed that raise the collective standard of protection.

The term gained relevance with the advancement of privacy regulations, which reinforce this right as a way of protecting the privacy and dignity of citizens in an increasingly digital world. Informational self-determination involves, for example, the right to consent or refuse the use of your data, access to stored information, request rectification or deletion and the possibility of portability of personal data to other services.

This principle goes beyond simple data protection, as it establishes a balance of power between individuals and organizations, promoting transparency and responsibility in the use of personal information. It also underpins the foundation of ethical practices in the era of the digital economy, where intensive use of data can directly impact fundamental rights such as freedom, equality and autonomy.

The rights that must be offered to data subjects include access to personal data, rectification of incorrect information, deletion of data, limitation of processing and portability. Furthermore, data subjects have the right to object to the use of their data for certain purposes, such as direct marketing, and to request detailed information about how their data is processed. To meet these rights, the website must provide an accessible channel, such as an online form or specific email address, accompanied by clear guidance on how users can exercise their rights.

Each privacy legislation establishes specific rights and requirements for their implementation, reflecting the cultural, economic and regulatory particularities of each country or region. For example, the GDPR in the European Union defines rights such as data portability and the right to be forgotten, allowing individuals to request the deletion of their information when it is no longer necessary for the original purpose of the processing. In Brazil, the LGPD requires express consent for various activities that involve data considered sensitive, ensuring greater transparency and control for the holder.

In Saudi Arabia, the Personal Data Protection Law (PDPL) imposes restrictions on the international transfer of data and requires that any collection or processing be done on a clear legal basis, emphasizing the protection of privacy in accordance with Islamic principles. India's Digital Personal Data Protection Act (DPDP), enacted in 2023, highlights data minimization and the obligation of accountability, requiring companies to protect personal information and offer simplified means for data subjects to exercise their rights.

Faced with these variations, companies must adjust their compliance processes and service channels to meet the requirements of the jurisdiction where they operate, ensuring regulatory compliance and strengthening user confidence.

The presence of a DPO (Data Protection Officer) on the website is a fundamental requirement in many regulations. The DPO acts as a point of contact for data subjects and regulatory authorities, ensuring compliance with privacy laws. On the website, the DPO's contact information, such as email and telephone, must be clearly available to facilitate user access and demonstrate transparency in the processing of personal data.

The absence of a DPO or a channel to serve cardholders can result in significant sanctions, including administrative fines and damage to the company's reputation. Furthermore, the absence of adequate channels can lead to distrust among users, negatively impacting business and making relationships with customers and partners difficult.

Carlos, a law student always aware of the latest developments in privacy and data protection, decided to test the right he had as a holder. He was curious to know how a large online store, where he regularly shopped, treated his personal information. When visiting the website, he found a simple form to request his data and quickly filled out the necessary information. All you had to do was include your registered email and a brief description of the order. To his surprise, in less than an hour, he received an email with a file containing all the requested information.

Excited by the speed, he opened the file immediately. However, when he started reading the data, he noticed something strange. The name on the report was Ana Beatriz and the content contained information such as purchase history, delivery addresses and even payment data. Carlos was alarmed. He, who was hoping to verify the use of his own data, had someone else's highly confidential information in his hands. "This isn't right," he thought. The store clearly had not implemented technical measures to verify the identity of the person placing the order.

Intrigued and somewhat indignant, Carlos decided to test something. He sent another request to the system, this time using a fictitious email he had just created. To his surprise, once again, he quickly received a report. This new file contained data from another customer, further exposing the severity of the problem. He realized that the store's system was completely automated, without any effective validation to confirm whether the requester was, in fact, the data owner.

Carlos contacted the store, explaining the critical flaw he had discovered. Initially, he was ignored, but when he mentioned that he was considering reporting the case to the data protection authority, he received a call from the legal department. The company admitted that the automated system had been designed to quickly serve cardholders, but neglected essential authentication measures in a rush to comply with regulations. Ultimately, the store reviewed the entire system and implemented rigorous checks such as document validation and multi-factor authentication.

Meanwhile, Carlos realized that his curiosity had exposed a serious problem. More than just seeking transparency, his request served as a warning about the importance of combining technology with responsibility. After all, in the race to fulfill privacy rights, neglecting security can turn a good intention into a major disaster.

Automation in serving data subjects brings significant benefits. It allows companies to process requests quickly, reducing operational costs and optimizing resources. However, when poorly implemented, this automation can introduce serious risks, such as exposing personal data to unauthorized people. Lack of proper authentication or validation flows can lead to privacy breaches that compromise customer trust and expose the organization to severe legal penalties.

The use of professional tools *data discovery* and identity verification is essential to ensure security and accuracy in automated service. Tools *data discovery* professionals, help to identify and catalog the personal data stored by the organization, allowing the information to be promptly located and delivered only to the correct holder. At the same time, identity verification solutions such as multi-factor authentication, biometrics or document validation ensure that the person requesting the data is, in fact, who they claim to be.

You can never send personal data to someone without being fully confident that it is the correct person.

Setting up a *workflow* well-structured service to holders is another critical component. A flow must include clear steps for receiving the request, validating identity, processing the data and responding to the subject. Using request management tools allows you to monitor and prioritize requests, as well as maintaining a history for future audits. That *workflow* it must be designed to ensure compliance with legal deadlines and minimize human intervention at points where errors or violations may occur.

Creating a privacy portal for users is another idea for a robust solution that centralizes and organizes service to data subjects. This portal may include a registration system with identity validation using the KYC method (*Know Your Customer*), using information already available in the company's user base. When integrated with internal platforms, the portal can facilitate data subject access to their data and management options, such as editing consents or requesting deletions. In addition to increasing efficiency, this approach promotes transparency and strengthens the relationship of trust between the company and its customers.

However, implementing a KYC system needs to consider current challenges, such as the use of deepfake to defraud identity verification processes. With advances in artificial intelligence, criminals are able to create highly realistic videos and images that imitate the faces, voices and even facial expressions of real individuals. This can be exploited to bypass facial recognition in online registrations, allowing fraudsters to create fake accounts or assume the identity of other people, compromising data security and the reliability of the privacy portal.

I'm Hong Kong[47], a group of scammers used deepfake technology to impersonate a company's chief financial officer and managed to trick a bank into transferring $35 million to fraudulent accounts. They faked the executive's voice so convincingly that no one suspected it.

It all started when criminals sent emails and made calls to the bank, pretending to be the CFO. They used artificial intelligence to imitate his voice perfectly, requesting urgent bank transfers. As the bank already had a relationship with the company and recognized the executive's voice, it processed the transfers without question.

Only after the real CFO discovered strange movements in the accounts was the scam revealed. Unfortunately, the scammers had already disappeared with the money.

To mitigate this risk, companies must adopt multiple authentication factors, combining biometrics with proof of life, such as detecting blinks or natural facial movements in real time. Additionally, advanced metadata and digital behavior analysis techniques can be applied to identify suspicious patterns and signs of synthetic manipulation. Integrating solutions that use machine learning to detect deepfakes in real time can significantly increase the effectiveness of KYC systems, ensuring that only legitimate users have access to their privacy rights and the management of their data.

Compliance with Data Subjects' Rights: When GDPR Became a Weapon

I've seen it all on my journey with privacy, but what happened in 2019 made me stop and think: what if a law designed to protect data became a way to expose it? A researcher from the University of Oxford, James Pavur, presented[48] at Black Hat something that moved me. He used the GDPR's "right of access" — the one anyone can invoke to ask for your information — to pretend to be his fiancée and request her data from dozens of companies in the UK and US. Result? One in four places turned over everything without checking who he was: travel history, credit card, even her full US Social Security number. This shows how complying with the rights of holders can become a risk if you are not careful.

His scheme was simple but clever. With a fake email in the format "first-middle-last-name@gmail.com" and a letter citing the GDPR's one-month deadline, he asked for everything they had on her. Some companies, like a British hotel chain and an American education firm, sent her complete lists of stays, high school grades, and even a criminal background report — without even asking for a decent document. For those who work with systems, this is a warning: never trust just what the user says. Set up a solid verification process, such as requiring an authenticated login or a scanned ID sent through a secure portal. I've seen teams skip this step out of laziness, but the service process requires protection, not just a quick response.

What impressed me was how big companies, like Tesco and American Airlines, did well, asking for a passport photo or doing a telephone interview, while smaller or medium-sized companies simply failed. One even accepted a bank statement that was almost completely erased, with only the name and address visible — imagine how easy that is to falsify. As an engineer, you can avoid this type of slip-up by using multi-factor authentication (MFA) on your fulfillment platforms or, at the very least, a decent CAPTCHA to filter automatic orders. Another idea is to log each request with tools like Splunk or ELK, to track who requested what and how it was verified. This way, you guarantee the right of access without opening the door to anyone.

In the end, Pavur's case — who, incidentally, had his fiancée's permission to take the test — is a personal reminder: meeting the rights of holders is not just about meeting deadlines, it's about protecting those who trust you. He managed to obtain 60 types of personal data from her, including passwords that still worked on other sites, because no one checked properly. One company even posted his letter online, exposing her name, address and phone number in an extra leak. So, here's the message: build systems that ask for proof of identity before releasing anything.

PRIVACY AND TRANSPARENCY POLICY

A good privacy policy works as a link to establish transparency and trust between the company and its users. It functions as an implicit contract that details how personal data is collected, used, stored and protected. In addition to meeting legal requirements imposed by regulations, a well-written policy demonstrates the organization's commitment to privacy, increasing the public's perception of responsibility and ethics.

But do we need to make the entire privacy policy available to users? In this case, we have a privacy notice mechanism available. The difference between a privacy policy and a privacy notice is the purpose and approach of each. The privacy policy is a more robust document that describes the organization's general principles and data processing practices, often made available internally. The privacy notice is more specific, aimed at specific data collection contexts, such as specific forms or functionalities, informing the user what information is being collected at that moment and for what purpose, generally available on the company's channels.

Offering users the possibility of comparing previous versions of the document and viewing what has been changed is a practice that reinforces transparency. This allows data subjects to understand how information processing has evolved and make informed decisions about continuing to share their data with the organization. Tools that highlight changes or direct links to previous versions are practical examples that promote clarity and confidence.

The Privacy Policy Dilemma

When I started working with privacy, I thought privacy policies were the key to giving data subjects control over their data — until I realized that no one reads them. An article from *The Washington Post*[49] 2022, written by Geoffrey Fowler, shed light on this in a way that made me rethink everything. He talks about how Twitter and Facebook tried to simplify their policies — Twitter even turned his into a game called *Twitter Data Dash*[50], at 4,500 words, while Facebook rewrote its for a high school level but stretched it to 12,000 words. Still, who has the time or patience for that? This made me see that the right to transparency is empty if people don't understand what they are consenting to.

The problem is not just the size, but what these policies hide under the carpet. Fowler argues that companies use these huge texts to justify collecting too much data, often without giving data subjects real options. I've been through this in projects: you think you're informing the user, but in reality you're just filling the gap. One way out is to reduce what you collect from the beginning — the famous principle of minimization. As an engineer, you can configure systems that only take what is necessary. For example, use short session cookies instead of persistent trackers, or adjust the backend to ask for explicit opt-ins on each extra collection. Thus, the holder does not need to decipher a book to have control.

The article cites a case that I highlight here: even with efforts like the *Data Dash*, companies do not solve the real obstacle — overload. Fowler suggests doing away with the idea that users must read policies and instead focusing on "disclosures" to regulators, letting protection come from less collection. This resonates with data subjects' right to choose: if I ask to access or delete my data, I want a system that listens to me, not bury me in text. A practical tip is to create simple data management interfaces — like a panel where the user sees everything you have with a "delete" button. In your code, use APIs like *Privacy Dashboard* from Google or something customized to show and delete data in real time.

Basically, what I learned from this reading is that fulfilling the rights of holders is not about throwing words in their faces — it's about giving real power. I have already configured systems thinking that a long policy was enough, but the *Post* showed me that this is an illusion. Companies like Twitter and Facebook can try, but as long as they collect everything and more, the holder is held hostage. So, here's the lesson: build software that nips the problem in the bud, limiting data and offering clear options. Use logs to track requests and ensure that deletions are quick — like a well-crafted SQL command that only clears what the user requested. This way, you actually respect the rights that the law promises.

A privacy notice should be objectively structured, covering the following main topics, such as:

1. Identification of the company responsible for data processing.
2. The purposes of data collection and the legal bases that justify the processing.
3. Detailed information about the data collected and how it is used.
4. Rights of holders and how to exercise them.
5. Sharing data with third parties, when applicable.
6. Security measures adopted to protect information.
7. Data retention period and criteria for deletion.
8. Contact information for support or questions. Accessible language and usable design help ensure that all users understand the content of the notice,

regardless of their level of technical knowledge.

CHECKLIST OF PRACTICAL ACTIONS

☐ I integrated privacy principles from the initial software design.

☐ I have set privacy defaults as the default setting on the system.

☐ I applied pseudonymization techniques to protect sensitive data during processing.

☐ Anonymize data whenever identification of the holder is not necessary.

☐ I reduced data collection to the minimum necessary for each purpose.

☐ Developed segregated architectures to store and process sensitive data.

☐ I only set cookies with the user's explicit consent.

☐ I have provided options for users to manage cookie preferences.

☐ Implemented a portal to handle data access and deletion requests.

☐ I updated and made the privacy policy available with transparency and clarity.

☐ Protect cloud data with encryption, access control and continuous monitoring.

☐ I obfuscated real data in test environments to avoid unnecessary exposure.

CHAPTER 3

Secure Development and Technical Compliance

Developing secure software aligned with technical privacy standards is a necessity in a scenario where personal data is constantly at risk. This chapter discusses how secure development techniques can be implemented to protect systems against vulnerabilities and ensure data integrity. We will explore techniques such as robust access control, applied encryption and the use of trusted libraries, as well as methodologies such as DevSecOps, which integrate security into all stages of development. Emphasis will be placed on the importance of aligning technical security with regulatory compliance, ensuring that software meets legal requirements without compromising its efficiency and usability.

SECURITY FUNDAMENTALS IN SOFTWARE DEVELOPMENT

Security in software development begins with a mindset of protection from system design, ensuring that security is not an afterthought, but an intrinsic component. This involves early identification of security requirements during the planning phase, considering potential threats and possible attack vectors. Threat models such as STRIDE[51] or FOLDER[52], can be used to map vulnerabilities and risks at different layers of the system, allowing developers to make informed decisions about the controls to be implemented.

Implementing secure coding practices is one of the cornerstones of mitigating vulnerabilities. This includes avoiding common flaws such as SQL injections, sensitive data exposure, and cross-site scripting by utilizing rigorous input and output validation, data sanitization, and parameterized query construction. Static code analysis tools can be integrated into the development pipeline to identify vulnerabilities in real time, while manual peer code reviews help detect flaws that automated tools may miss.

Lucas was an experienced developer known for his ability

to solve complex code problems. He worked for an e-commerce startup called FastBuy, which was growing quickly and attracting more and more customers. One day, while reviewing the sales dashboard, he noticed something strange: there was an anomalous spike in access to the administration system, all originating from an unknown IP address. Intrigued, he began to investigate.

While analyzing the database logs, Lucas noticed that unauthorized SQL commands were being executed. An attacker had exploited a vulnerability in the login system. The security team confirmed: FastBuy had been the victim of an SQL injection. The attacker inserted malicious code into the username input field, where the system did not sanitize the entries before running database queries. The command was something like: admin' OR '1'='1. This injection forced the SQL query to always return true, granting administrative access to the system.

The failure was traced to a snippet of code in the backend, where the application directly concatenated user-supplied values to SQL queries. The vulnerable code looked something like this, in Java programming language

String query = "SELECT * FROM users WHERE username = '" + username + "' AND password = '" + password + "'";

ResultSet rs = stmt.executeQuery(query);

The attacker used this loophole to bypass authentication, gaining access to sensitive customer data and purchase history.

Lucas knew that The first step would be to fix the code to prevent malicious input from being processed as SQL commands. He implemented parameterized queries using Prepared Statements, which separated the data from the SQL statements, making it impossible for the attacker to manipulate the query. The updated code looked like this:

```
String query = "SELECT * FROM users WHERE username = ?
AND password = ?";
PreparedStatement              pstmt              =
connection.prepareStatement(query);
pstmt.setString(1, username);
pstmt.setString(2, password);
ResultSet rs = pstmt.executeQuery();
```

Additionally, Lucas and the team configured an input validation layer to reject suspicious characters directly on the frontend, added a strong password policy, and integrated a web application firewall (WAF) solution to detect and block future SQL injection attempts. They also began using centralized logs to monitor unusual access and activity, enabling faster response to potential incidents.

The vulnerability was fixed and the systems became more secure. The incident served as a watershed moment for FastBuy. The entire team adopted a proactive security stance, constantly reviewing code and implementing best practices. Lucas turned the disaster into a learning experience, leading internal workshops to teach colleagues the dangers of SQL injection and how to avoid it. For him, true success was not just protecting the system, but empowering everyone around him to do the same.

Managing dependencies and external libraries ends up being critical to software security. Obsolete libraries or libraries with known vulnerabilities can be exploited by attackers to compromise system integrity. Therefore, actively monitor the versions used, apply security updates as they become available, and audit the reliability of sources before incorporating any dependencies. Package managers such as Maven and Gradle can be configured to automatically scan libraries for vulnerabilities, reducing the risk of exposure.

Applying encryption is essential to protect data both at rest and in transit. Modern algorithms, such as AES and RSA, must be used to guarantee the confidentiality and integrity of information. Correctly implementing TLS certificates to secure communication between clients and servers can help prevent man-in-the-middle attacks. Furthermore, encryption key management must be treated rigorously, using secure solutions for storage and periodic rotation, minimizing the possibility of compromise.

Finally, security in software development must be continually assessed through testing, such as penetration testing and dynamic security assessments. These tests simulate real attacks to identify weaknesses in the system before they can be exploited. Additionally, post-deployment monitoring should be standard practice, with log analysis tools and intrusion detection systems integrated into the production environment. This proactive approach ensures that security is not static, but an evolutionary practice that adapts to changing threats.

The Ladders Case[53]: When an oversight exposed 13 million CVs

Just imagine: you are a developer taking care of a system full of personal data, such as resumes with names, emails and even work histories. Then, in 2019, Ladders, an American website famous for high-level jobs, left 13.7 million user records exposed because of a silly error. An Elasticsearch database hosted on AWS was open, without a password, for anyone to access. This included not only candidates, but also 379,000 recruiters. The worst? It was a gold mine of personal information, like addresses and phone numbers, all available for years before someone noticed. Moral of the story: safety is not optional, and one mistake can turn into a nightmare.

What happened was simple: someone forgot to lock the door. Elasticsearch database didn't have basic authentication, something you set up in minutes. To avoid this type of error, always check whether access to your database is restricted. In

AWS, for example, you can use IP rules in the security group or put a password in Elasticsearch — just change the configuration file or use the panel to activate. Another golden tip: never trust that the default configuration will save you. Ladders thought it was OK because AWS said the service was "secure," but without a password or restriction, it's like leaving the key in the front door.

When a GDI Foundation researcher found this bank open, he notified TechCrunch, who in turn notified Ladders. Within an hour, access was blocked — but it was too late to know who had entered first. To avoid falling for this, it's worth running tools like nmap or Shodan from time to time to see if your servers are exposed on the internet. Another idea is to set up basic monitoring, like CloudWatch on AWS, to warn you if something strange is happening in the traffic. And, seriously, document everything: who accesses it, how it accesses it, and what is released. If Ladders had done this, it might not have made the news.

Ladders' CEO blamed a possible "theft", but the hole was deeper: lack of basic care. To avoid repeating this mistake, think about security from the beginning of the project. Use the principle of least privilege — only release what you need, to as few people as possible. And test, test a lot: simulate an attack with a tool like Burp Suite to see where your system could leak.

SECURE CODING PRACTICES AND VULNERABILITY PREVENTION

Secure coding requires programmers to integrate privacy as a priority from the beginning of development. This means considering how personal data will be processed, stored and protected, while avoiding introducing vulnerabilities that could be exploited. For example, when dealing with sensitive data, it is important to implement strong encryption and restrict access to only those who truly need it. Additionally, developers should avoid insecure practices such as storing data directly in code or configuration files. These measures not only increase security, but also ensure that the system respects privacy principles.

Security by design principles directly complement privacy by design. While the first focuses on building resilient systems against attacks, the second focuses on protecting personal data from design. Both share fundamental values, such as minimizing risks and anticipating problems. For example, security by design emphasizes the use of multi-factor authentication and granular access control, while privacy by design advocates collecting minimal data and anonymizing it when possible. Together, these principles create an ecosystem where privacy and security go hand in hand.

The principles of secure development are fundamental guides for creating systems that are robust and resilient against threats. Each principle promotes practices that minimize vulnerabilities and maximize the protection of systems and data. Here are the main ones:

1. **Defense in depth**: Implement multiple layers of security to protect systems if one is compromised.

2. **Least privilege**: Grant only the strictly necessary permissions to each user, system or process.

3. **Strict input validation**: Treat all external input as potentially malicious and validate it before processing.

4. **Security by default**: Configure the system to operate securely, requiring explicit actions to be taken to enable less secure functionality.

5. **Attack surface minimization**: Reduce the system's entry points and interaction with the external environment as much as possible.

6. **Fail safe**: Design the system so that it maintains security even in the event of failures or errors.

7. **Obscurity security as an additional layer**: Do not rely exclusively on obscurity to protect the system, but use it as a complement to other measures.

8. **Secure session management and authentication**: Use strong authentication, secure active sessions, and implement expiration and renewal policies.

9. **Runtime protection**: Monitor system behavior to detect and respond to anomalies or intrusions in real

time.

10. **Continuous auditing and monitoring**: Record and analyze activities to identify improper access, fraud or security breaches.

11. **Secure development lifecycle**: Integrate security practices into every stage of development, from planning to maintenance.

12. **Education and awareness**: Empower developers and teams to continually understand and apply security best practices.

A core practice in security by design is adopting the principle of least privilege, ensuring that each component or user has only the permissions necessary to perform its functions. This is especially relevant when considered in parallel to privacy by design, which advocates restricting access to sensitive data. For example, in an e-commerce system, only finance should have access to payment information, while customer support can handle less critical data such as order status. This segregation of responsibilities drastically reduces the impact of a possible breach.

Vulnerability prevention starts with rigorous validation of data inputs. SQL injections, malicious scripts, and other attacks exploit flaws in how the system processes information provided by users. In addition to protecting the code against these threats, validation is also a privacy issue, as it prevents sensitive data from being improperly extracted or manipulated. Using modern, actively maintained libraries to sanitize inputs and outputs is a practice that promotes both security and respect for privacy.

Finally, continuous testing and audits are imperative to ensure that secure coding practices and design principles are effectively applied. Automated tools like vulnerability scanners can quickly identify issues, while manual testing helps validate implemented controls. The constant alignment between security and privacy, in addition to protecting data and systems, demonstrates an ethical commitment to users and promotes trust in an increasingly digital world.

The ResumeLooters Case and the Stolen Data

I've worked on systems that seemed secure until someone showed me how a silly mistake could turn into a disaster — and the case with ResumeLooters is exactly that. In 2024, the *SecurityWeek*[54] published a Group-IB alert about a group that, between November and December 2023, stole more than two million emails and personal data from 65 websites, using mainly SQL injection attacks. They targeted retail and recruitment websites, taking names, phone numbers, dates of birth and even employment histories of candidates.

What caught my attention was the simplicity of the attack. ResumeLooters used open source tools to inject malicious SQL commands and suck up entire databases — nearly 2.2 million rows, more than 500,000 of them from job sites. Some attacks have gone further, with XSS scripts hidden in fake profiles or resumes, tricking administrators into stealing credentials. To avoid this type of scam, I always say: sanitize everything that comes in. Configure your queries with parameters in the backend — type PreparedStatement in Java or bind_param in PHP — to block injections. And if you work with forms, use a Content Security Policy (CSP) on the server to limit external scripts.

Group-IB pointed out that the group sold this data in Chinese-language Telegram groups, reaching sites in Asia, but also in the US, Brazil and elsewhere. This reminds me of how much the right to deletion or access is compromised when data escapes — imagine a data subject asking to delete something that is already on the illegal market? One lesson I took from this is to always test your defenses. Use tools like SQLMap [55]to simulate attacks and see where your system might give way. Another idea is to encrypt personal data in the database with AES-256, so even if it gets leaked, it's just a bunch of meaningless numbers without the key. It's a simple step that saves a lot of headaches.

Basically, this case shows that meeting the rights of holders is not just responding to requests — it is preventing them from needing to chase losses. ResumeLooters took advantage of "bad database management practices," as Group-IB put it, and I've seen this in projects: people leaving doors open out of laziness or lack of knowledge. So, the message is: invest in security from the beginning. Set up logs with something like the ELK Stack to track strange access and have a clear process to quickly delete data when asked. Protecting data subjects' data is more than complying with the law — it's ensuring that they don't become targets because of our error.

DEVSECOPS: INTEGRATING SECURITY INTO THE DEVELOPMENT CYCLE

DevSecOps is an approach that integrates security directly into the software development cycle, promoting collaboration between developers, operations teams and security experts. Unlike traditional methods, where security was treated as a post-development process, DevSecOps incorporates security practices from conception to continuous deployment. This integration enables early detection of vulnerabilities and rapid response to emerging threats, aligning the rapid pace of development with the need for robust systems and data protection.

In terms of infrastructure, DevSecOps emphasizes automation to ensure environments are configured in a consistent and secure manner. Tools like Terraform and Ansible help provision infrastructure as code, allowing configurations to be versioned and audited, reducing human error. Services like Cloudflare also offer protection against DDoS attacks, a web application firewall, and traffic optimization, ensuring that infrastructure is protected and operational, even under adverse conditions.

In cloud models, the impact on privacy and security varies depending on the type of service used: IaaS (Infrastructure as a Service), PaaS (Platform as a Service) or SaaS (Software as a Service). In the IaaS model, such as that offered by AWS or Azure, the responsibility for data and infrastructure security largely falls on the customer, who must implement practices such as network segmentation and access controls. In PaaS, where the provider manages the application layer and the customer focuses on development, it is essential to ensure that processed data is encrypted and that APIs are protected against unauthorized access. In SaaS, such as Google Workspace or Salesforce, privacy is strongly impacted by the way data is stored and shared, requiring providers to offer robust security and transparency settings.

Another aspect of DevSecOps is continuous vulnerability monitoring at all levels, from code to infrastructure. Scanning tools like Snyk and SonarQube identify flaws in libraries and dependencies, while services like AWS GuardDuty monitor suspicious activity in cloud environments. This proactive approach is complemented by secure CI/CD pipelines, where each deployment step is audited and subjected to automated security testing, ensuring that only secure code reaches the production environment.

During system use, logs are fundamental tools for system operation and maintenance, recording information about events, errors and activities that occur in the IT infrastructure. For example, for functions such as debugging, auditing, and security monitoring, logs allow teams to identify anomalies and troubleshoot problems efficiently. However, logs also pose a significant privacy risk when they are not configured or managed properly. Critical information, such as user credentials, authentication tokens or personal data, can be stored incorrectly, making them vulnerable to unauthorized access or leaks. Implementing practices such as log sanitization, data masking, and encryption help balance operational utility with privacy protection, ensuring that only relevant and secure information is recorded and accessed.

Rogério was an experienced infrastructure manager, known for his ability to keep large systems running like Swiss clocks. He led the IT team at a fintech company called FinSecure, which offered financial solutions to thousands of customers. The routine was challenging but under control, until the day an urgent notification arrived in her email: a customer had requested details about how their data was being handled, and an external auditor was checking the company's privacy compliance.

Rogério quickly called on his team to review the system logs, a common practice to identify possible points of concern. When he opened the files, something caught his attention: the logs were full of personal information. Logins, email addresses and even financial transaction data were being explicitly recorded in the logs. "How did this go unnoticed?" he thought. He knew that if these logs fell into the wrong hands, the impact would be catastrophic for both customers and the company's reputation.

Determined to solve the problem, Rogério began an investigation to understand the origin of the data in the logs. He discovered that one of the authentication systems, implemented hastily during a platform expansion, was configured to log all requests and completed responses on each login attempt. While useful for debugging, this configuration completely neglected users' privacy. The code was storing authentication tokens and credentials in open text, exposing critical data without any layer of protection.

Rogério worked tirelessly to correct the error. First, he instructed the team to apply sanitization techniques to the logs, ensuring that only information essential for monitoring was recorded. Using a log management solution such as ELK Stack, they implemented rules that masked data before it was written. Additionally, they enabled end-to-end encryption for the log files and strictly restricted access to the logs, allowing only authorized users to view them.

With the measures implemented, Rogério carried out a complete audit of the system to ensure that no other functionality was exposing personal data. In the end, the external auditor praised the actions taken by the team, highlighting the speed and efficiency in mitigating the problem. For Rogério, the incident was a warning that even common practices, such as generating logs, could turn into significant risks if privacy was not integrated into the infrastructure from the beginning. He then decided to adopt a "privacy by default" policy across all company operations, ensuring that mistakes like this would never happen again.

DevSecOps also transforms organizational culture, promoting security awareness across all teams involved in development. Regular training and incident simulations help create a collective security mindset, where each team member understands their role in protecting systems and data. This approach tends to help you in a scenario where the complexity of systems and the sophistication of attacks are constantly evolving, demanding solutions that are both technical and human.

DATA PROTECTION IN CLOUD ENVIRONMENTS

Cloud service models — Infrastructure as a Service (IaaS), Platform as a Service (PaaS) and Software as a Service (SaaS) — have distinct implications for data privacy and security, directly influencing protection responsibilities. In IaaS, like AWS EC2 or Azure Virtual Machines, the provider takes care of the hardware... but you are in charge of the operating system, the apps and the data... This requires the engineer to configure firewalls, segment networks with VPCs (Virtual Private Clouds) and encrypt disks with tools such as AWS EBS encryption, as the responsibility for privacy falls largely on the user. For example, a poorly configured S3 bucket with public access can expose sensitive data, as has happened in real leak incidents. In PaaS, such as Google App Engine or Heroku, the provider assumes more layers (OS and runtime), but the customer must protect the data processed in the applications — unprotected APIs or lack of encryption in traffic (e.g.: poorly configured TLS) can compromise personal information, requiring endpoint validation. In SaaS, such as Salesforce or Google Workspace, customer control is minimal, and privacy depends on the provider's policies, such as data sharing or retention settings; Here, the risk is in blindly trusting the vendor without reviewing permissions or enabling MFA (multi-factor authentication).

The choice of model directly impacts compliance strategies. In IaaS, flexibility allows you to implement custom solutions such as AES-256 encryption at rest and keys managed by AWS KMS, but requires effort to audit access logs with tools like CloudTrail, ensuring traceability of breaches. In PaaS, privacy can be strengthened with good development practices, such as sanitizing inputs to avoid data injections and using environment variables for credentials, but the engineer must monitor third-party dependencies that can introduce vulnerabilities — a common case is the use of outdated libraries in Docker containers. In SaaS, security depends on provided settings, such as restricting access to documents in Google Drive or setting automatic deletion policies, but a lack of transparency about where data is stored (e.g. jurisdictions outside the EU) can complicate compliance with international transfers. In all models, the integration of tools such as AWS GuardDuty or Azure Security Center for continuous monitoring is an important step, but the level of control and responsibility varies, requiring the engineer to adapt privacy practices to the chosen model, always prioritizing the principle of minimization and proactive protection.

When configuring *buckets* of storage, take care to restrict public access, defining specific permissions for each user or application that needs to interact with these resources. Additionally, it is recommended to enable access logs and implement versioning policies, ensuring that any changes to data can be tracked and rolled back. Databases must be configured with strong authentication, such as the use of digital certificates, and located in private subnets, separate from public internet access. Virtual machines, in turn, must be associated with security groups with restricted entry and exit rules, minimizing exposure to unnecessary ports.

Another important aspect of configuration involves the use of *firewalls* and virtual private networks to secure communication between services. Implementing restrictions based on IP or geographic locations for remote access is a practice that significantly reduces the risk of unauthorized access. Solutions such as VPNs or private link services can be used to securely connect sensitive resources, while using up-to-date operating systems and applications reduces the attack surface. Default settings must be reviewed immediately after resource provisioning, ensuring that only strictly necessary functionalities are enabled.

Data encryption in the cloud is essential to guarantee the confidentiality and integrity of information, both at rest and in transit. For data at rest, the use of cloud providers' native encryption technologies, such as AES-256, protects data stored on disks, databases, or buckets. Secure encryption key management is another critical point. Tools such as AWS KMS, Azure Key Vault and Google Cloud KMS allow keys to be managed centrally, offering detailed control over who can access and use these keys, as well as automatic rotation and usage log generation capabilities.

For data in transit, communication between clients and servers must be protected using secure protocols such as TLS (Transport Layer Security). Properly configuring digital certificates and enabling HTTPS on all public interfaces helps prevent man-in-the-middle attacks. Furthermore, it is important to regularly check that certificates are valid and up to date. In the case of services that depend on APIs, the application of payload encryption and strong authentication in communication between components contributes to a more secure environment.

Access control and identity management are essential for protecting cloud resources from unauthorized access. The implementation of IAM (Identity and Access Management) policies allows access to be granted based on the principle of least privilege, ensuring that users and applications only have the permissions necessary to perform their functions. Role-based policies, known as RBAC (Role-Based Access Control), help organize and simplify the assignment of permissions, while attribute-based policies (ABAC) can be used for more complex scenarios.

Another important element is enabling multi-factor authentication (MFA) for all users accessing critical cloud resources. This adds an extra layer of security, making attacks based on compromised credentials more difficult. Using federated identities to integrate external systems and enable single sign-on (SSO) can also reduce complexity and increase security. Additionally, the periodic rotation of credentials and programmatic access keys, combined with continuous monitoring of authentication logs, helps mitigate risks associated with poor identity management practices.

Activity monitoring and auditing are essential for detecting and responding to security incidents in cloud environments. Tools such as AWS CloudTrail, Azure Monitor or Google Cloud Operations Suite provide detailed visibility into resource access and changes. These tools record activities such as login attempts, modifications to security policies, and interactions with APIs, allowing administrators to identify suspicious or unauthorized usage patterns.

Analysis of these logs should be automated whenever possible, using configurable alerts to identify anomalous behavior in real time. Integration with security information and event management (SIEM) systems such as Splunk or Elastic Security can consolidate information from multiple sources, providing a centralized view of activities and accelerating incident response. Regular audits of permissions and configurations are also recommended to ensure that configuration drift does not occur over time.

Protecting against leaks and insecure configurations requires a proactive approach to identifying vulnerabilities and fixing issues before they are exploited. Solutions such as AWS Macie, Azure Security Center or Google Security Command Center use machine learning to detect anomalous behavior and locate inappropriately stored sensitive data. These services can help identify inadvertent public configurations, such as exposed storage buckets or overly broad permissions on databases.

Additionally, it is essential to implement data loss prevention (DLP) mechanisms, configuring rules that monitor traffic and block unauthorized sharing of information. Security tools can also be configured to regularly check the configurations of all cloud resources, issuing alerts or automatically patching detected vulnerabilities. This ensures an extra layer of protection and helps maintain the integrity of the environment over time.

Finally, carrying out hardening actions are important. Hardening is the process of strengthening the security of systems, servers, networks and applications by reducing the attack surface and minimizing exploitable vulnerabilities. It involves applying practices and settings such as disabling unnecessary services and ports, removing default or outdated accounts, configuring restricted access permissions, and applying security updates regularly. Additionally, hardening includes implementing policies such as multi-factor authentication, data encryption, and audit logs to track activity. Automated tools such as Ansible or Chef can be used to standardize and automate hardening on a large scale, ensuring consistency and compliance in complex environments. The ultimate goal is to create a secure base, reducing the impact of possible internal and external threats as much as possible.

DATA OBFUSCATION TECHNIQUES FOR TESTING ENVIRONMENTS

Data obfuscation is the process of modifying data to make it unrecognizable or unusable to unauthorized parties while maintaining, where possible, its usefulness for specific purposes such as testing and development. This concept is especially important in IT environments where production data cannot be exposed in less secure environments, such as testing or development environments. Obfuscation acts as a layer of protection by hiding critical data, reducing the risk of breach and allowing safe use in system simulations or training.

On a sunny morning, Sofia, a data engineer known for her creativity, was called to an emergency meeting at TechSecure, the technology company where she worked. The reason? A catastrophic data breach in a test environment had compromised data for thousands of users. The data included names, addresses, credit card numbers and even medical histories. All because an analyst, in a hurry to finish a project, used production data without any layer of protection.

The impact was devastating. The press reported the incident as "one of the biggest technological oversights of the year".

Customer confidence plummeted, and Sofia knew her team had a responsibility to right the wrong. During the meeting, while some suggested suspending the use of data, Sofia didn't just want to put out the fire: she suggested changing the game, completely changing how the company handled data, incorporating advanced obfuscation techniques.

Sofia started a task force. First, it identified all vulnerable points in data pipelines. He found that developers often had unrestricted access to production bases. In response, he implemented a masking system that replaces real data with fictitious values. A name like "Carlos Silva" became "João Ferreira", but the format and quality were maintained, allowing risk-free testing.

For the most critical information, like credit card numbers, Sofia has adopted tokenization. It used a highly secure digital vault to store the original data and generated unique tokens for use in test systems. These tokens were irreversible in the development environment, ensuring that no one could reverse the protection.

Sofia also set up an ETL pipeline with Python and the Faker library: fake.name() generated fictitious names like 'João Ferreira' instead of 'Carlos Silva'. For tokenization, it integrated a HashiCorp Vault vault.

But it wasn't easy. The team faced resistance. Some developers complained that obfuscated data was less "practical" for testing. Sofia patiently organized workshops to show how these techniques protected users' privacy without compromising the quality of the work. Little by little, the culture began to change. The team came to see data protection as an element of innovation, not an obstacle.

One year later, TechSecure has not only recovered but has become a reference in data security. Other companies were looking for Sofia to implement similar solutions. Experience has shown that data obfuscation is not just a technique, but a demonstration of respect and commitment to users. For Sofia, real success came when a young intern told her, "Before, I just wanted to finish projects quickly. Now, I understand that every line of code can protect lives."

Although often confused with anonymization and pseudonymization, obfuscation has a broader objective, focused on security in specific contexts. Anonymization permanently removes the identification of the holder, making reversion impossible, while pseudonymization replaces direct identifiers with indirect ones, maintaining the possibility of re-identification through controlled access. Obfuscation, in turn, can encompass both, depending on the techniques used, but is generally focused on temporary and controlled scenarios.

There are several ways to do obfuscation in different programming languages. Faker is an open-source Python library widely used to generate realistic fictional data. It is designed to create synthetic information that imitates real data, such as names, addresses, telephone numbers, emails, identification numbers, among others, without exposing personal data. It is particularly useful in development and testing scenarios where it is necessary to populate databases or simulate realistic interactions without violating privacy.

As an example, below I demonstrate what a source code focusing on obfuscation would look like using the Faker library. I added some comments to the code to make it easier to understand so you can look for similar techniques for your situation.

```
from faker import Faker
import random

# Initialize Faker with a generic locale (American English for
example)
fake = Faker('en_US')
```

```python
# Dummy original data to simulate a real record
original_data = {
    "name": "John Doe",
    "email": "john.doe@example.com",
    "id_number": "123-45-6789", # Format similar to an SSN
(US)
    "phone": "+1-202-555-1234"
}

# Function to mask data
def mask_data(data):
    masked_data = {}

    # Mask the name with a fictitious name generated by Faker
    masked_data["name"] = fake.name()

    # Mask the email with a fictitious email
    masked_data["email"] = fake.email()

    # Mask the identification number (e.g. SSN-like) with a
generated number
    # Keeping the format XXX-XX-XXXX

    masked_id = f"{random.randint(100, 999)}-
{random.randint(10, 99)}-{random.randint(1000, 9999)}"
    masked_data["id_number"] = masked_id

    # Mask the phone with a fictitious number in international
format
    masking_data["phone"] = fake.phone_number()

    return masked_data

# Apply masking
masked_data = mask_data(original_data)

# Display results
print("Original Data:")
```

```
for key, value in original_data.items():
    print(f"{key}: {value}")

print("\nMasked Data:")
for key, value in masked_data.items():
    print(f"{key}: {value}")

# Example of possible output:
# Original Data:
# name: John Doe
# email: john.doe@example.com
# id_number: 123-45-6789
# phone: +1-202-555-1234
#
# Masked Data:
# nome: Emily Johnson
# email: michael77@example.org
# id_number: 547-82-1934
# phone: 1-832-555-9876
```

Data masking is one of the most used techniques, replacing data that can identify someone with fictitious values, but which preserve structural and semantic characteristics. For example, a real name can be replaced by a fictitious name generated by algorithms that respect cultural and linguistic standards. This method is highly efficient in testing environments that require plausible data to simulate real interactions without compromising privacy.

Tokenization is another powerful approach, which replaces personal data with unique identifiers called tokens. These tokens are generated and managed securely, while the original data remains in a highly controlled environment, such as a data vault. This allows test systems to process the tokens without having access to the original data, adding a significant layer of protection.

Randomization uses random values to replace the original data, breaking any possibility of association with the data subjects. For example, in a database containing addresses, each address can be replaced with a randomly generated code. Shuffling reorganizes values within a data set, preserving plausibility but eliminating direct correlations. For example, shuffling addresses between different records.

Tools such as Delphix and IBM InfoSphere Optim offer solutions for data obfuscation, enabling masking, tokenization and other techniques with high efficiency. Open-source tools like ARX are also popular for smaller-scale projects. Languages like Python offer libraries like Faker, which generates realistic fictional data for specific scenarios, and Java also has libraries widely used for this purpose, such as Apache Commons Text, JFairy, and OpenPseudonymiser.

Integrating obfuscation into ETL pipelines is important to ensure data is handled before it enters test environments. Automation in the obfuscation process reduces manual intervention, ensuring consistency and minimizing human errors. This can be done using custom scripts or dedicated tools integrated into the data processing flow.

Generating synthetic data is an advanced alternative to completely replacing real data in testing. Using machine learning algorithms, it is possible to create datasets that replicate patterns and behaviors of the original data without exposing them. This is especially useful in complex scenarios that require large volumes of data.

After obfuscation, validate the quality of the processed data. This includes ensuring that data maintains consistency, referential integrity, and usefulness for testing. Automated tools and manual validations help detect issues that could compromise functionality or test effectiveness.

The application of obfuscation varies across industries. In the financial sector, it is used to protect customer data in credit simulations; in healthcare, to anonymize medical records used in research. Adopting best practices, such as documenting processes and avoiding excessive obfuscation that makes data useless, will help you balance privacy and functionality in your project.

USE OF THIRD-PARTY APIS

Using third-party APIs is a common practice in modern software development, allowing the integration of advanced functionality without the need to build solutions from scratch. However, incorporating these APIs requires special attention to security, as they can introduce vulnerabilities if not properly evaluated and monitored. It is essential to check the vendor's reputation, review security documentation, and ensure that the API complies with data protection standards and good development practices.

One of the main concerns when using third-party APIs is the exposure of sensitive data. These APIs often require the sharing of critical information, such as authentication tokens or personal data, which can pose a risk if the communication is not adequately encrypted. Therefore, implement security mechanisms, such as the use of HTTPS protocols and the validation of digital certificates, to ensure that data travels securely between systems.

Furthermore, updating and maintaining third-party APIs are aspects that require continuous attention. Vendors may release new versions to fix vulnerabilities or improve functionality, and it is the development team's responsibility to ensure integrations are always up to date. Lack of updates can result in security breaches, especially if the API in question is discontinued or no longer receives technical support.

To consult CVE's (Common Vulnerabilities and Exposures), the developer must access reliable databases, such as the official

CVE Miter website[56] or the NVD[57], which detail known vulnerabilities. Use specific CVE identifiers or keywords related to the technologies you are using, such as libraries, frameworks, or operating systems. Stay up to date with RSS feeds or automated alerts to monitor for new vulnerabilities that may affect your dependencies. Additionally, integrate vulnerability analysis tools like OWASP Dependency-Check or Snyk into your development pipeline to proactively identify and fix security holes.

Another critical point is evaluating the impact that a third-party API can have on system performance and stability. Poorly designed APIs or those with scalability issues can compromise the user experience and even cause cascading failures. Therefore, it is recommended to perform rigorous testing, including load and security assessments, before integrating an API into the production environment.

Finally, it is important to establish contracts with API providers, defining responsibilities in case of security breaches or service interruptions. Transparency in the supplier's privacy and security policies, as well as the existence of an incident response plan, are factors that must be considered when choosing a third-party API, as what matters in these cases is to minimize or eliminate risks and ensure that the use of these tools contributes to the security and efficiency of the software developed.

Let's imagine a scenario that serves as a warning to all software engineering teams. In 2022, Meta Platforms Ireland Limited, Facebook's parent company, faced a fine[58] of €265 million applied by the Irish Data Protection Commission. The reason? A flaw in its contact import tools on Facebook and Instagram, which resulted in the unauthorized extraction of personal data from more than 500 million users, later made available on the internet.

The investigation revealed that between May 2018 and September 2019, contact import tools allowed third parties to obtain users' personal information without proper consent.

This breach highlighted the importance of incorporating data protection measures from the design phase and by default.

For software engineering teams, this incident reinforces the need to implement security and privacy measures from the beginning of the development of any tool or functionality. Failure to do so not only compromises users' trust, but can also result in financial penalties and damage to the company's reputation.

The CrowdStrike Case: When an API Exposes More Than It Should

I've already integrated third-party APIs into projects thinking that everything was under control, until seeing cases like what happened with CrowdStrike in 2024 made me rethink. A hacker called USDoD, known for leaks like the FBI's InfraGard, scraped and published a list of 103,000 lines of CrowdStrike Indicators of Compromise (IoCs), straight from *Falcon portal*, on a forum called Breach Forums. It was a 53MB CSV file with hashes, details of the Mispadu malware and even tactics from the SAMBASPIDER group — data that companies use to protect themselves, but that fell into the wrong hands. This made me realize how much of a risk relying on external APIs can be if you don't keep an eye on it.

But look how this leak happened. CrowdStrike said there was no breach in its systems, but that the data was available to "tens of thousands" of customers and partners via API or portal. USDoD simply scraped everything, probably with a script that pulled line by line from a public or poorly protected interface. For those who use third-party APIs, as I have done many times, the tip is clear: limit access. Set up API keys with minimal permissions — in CrowdStrike's case, they could have used short-expiration token authentication or request quotas. A simple rate limiting, like 100 calls per hour, would have already made this massive scraping difficult.

The leaked list had everything: MD5, SHA-1 and SHA-256

hashes, attack phases like "Delivery" and "Installation", and even MITER ATT&CK techniques like credential capture. I look at this and think: if you depend on a third-party API for threat intelligence, like CrowdStrike, you need to audit what it returns. Use tools like Postman to test calls and see if sensitive data is too exposed.

PRIVACY ON IOT DEVICES (INTERNET OF THINGS)

The exponential growth of IoT devices has brought significant advances in several areas, such as healthcare, transportation and home automation. However, this connectivity has also raised critical privacy concerns. Many IoT devices collect sensitive data, such as location, usage patterns and biometric information, without transparency for users. Ensuring the privacy of these devices requires an approach that combines user-centered design, robust security practices, and compliance with technical standards that protect data throughout its entire journey, from collection to storage.

Encryption is one of the main layers of protection for communications between IoT devices. Secure protocols such as TLS and DTLS are often used to establish encrypted channels, protecting data from interception during transmission. Additionally, using asymmetric keys for initial authentication and periodically renewing these keys helps mitigate man-in-the-middle attacks. IoT devices with limited resources, such as small sensors, can adopt lightweight algorithms, such as ECC (Elliptic Curve Cryptography), which offer a high level of security with low computational demand.

Managing consent in IoT environments is a unique challenge because many devices do not have traditional interfaces such as screens or browsers. To resolve this issue, manufacturers are expected to develop alternative consent methods, such as interfaces in mobile applications or voice commands. Furthermore, it must be ensured that users can clearly understand what data is being collected, what it will be used for, and with whom it will be shared. Consent management tools can be integrated into IoT platforms to give users continuous control over their preferences.

Vulnerabilities in IoT devices are a constant threat, with notorious examples such as botnet attacks that exploited misconfigured devices to carry out massive DDoS attacks. Common issues include unchanged default credentials, lack of firmware updates, and unsecured communications. Mitigating these vulnerabilities requires proactive measures, such as requiring password changes on first use, enabling automatic software updates, and implementing multi-factor authentication for administrative access. Regular penetration testing and security reviews should be performed to identify and fix weaknesses before they are exploited.

Ultimately, privacy in IoT devices depends not only on technologies, but also on greater awareness on the part of manufacturers and users. Companies should adopt a privacy by design approach, minimizing data collection and storing only what is necessary. For users, education on how to securely configure devices and regularly review permissions will definitely reduce risks in your project. In an increasingly connected world, privacy on IoT devices is both a collective responsibility and a technical issue.

The Case of Hacked Pacemakers: APIs and the Risk to the Heart

I've always found it fascinating how third-party APIs can connect systems, but I never imagined it could go so far as to touch someone's heartstrings — literally. An article[59] , by Aditya Kapoor and colleagues, made me think of this when remembering an episode of *Homeland* 2012, where a hacker kills the US vice president by speeding up his wireless pacemaker.

It sounds like fiction, but security experts, like those cited by Kapoor in a 2020 study, show that implantable medical devices, or CIEDs, such as pacemakers and defibrillators, are vulnerable to attacks via APIs or wireless connections. In 2007, Dick Cheney's cardiologist turned off the Wi-Fi on his pacemaker out of fear of this — and I understand why: poorly protected APIs can open doors that no one wants to see wide open.

What concerned me was how these devices rely on APIs to send data to doctors via Bluetooth or Wi-Fi. The study explains that modern CIEDs use RF-link or even smartphones to transmit information such as device status or cardiac events, often via third-party APIs on home monitors or hospital systems. However, these connections do not have regular security updates — unlike your cell phone — because any change requires recertification by the FDA or other agencies in each country. I've seen third-party APIs in projects where security was an Achilles heel, so my tip is clear: restrict access. Use strong authentication, such as OAuth 2.0 with short-lived tokens, and configure firewalls to block calls outside of a trusted network. This cuts the risk of someone intercepting data or commands with a software-defined radio (SDR), as hackers have already tested in labs.

In this case in the article, experts used simple hardware and device manuals to take control or steal data, while Kapoor details attacks such as "battery drain" or telemetry manipulation that could shut down a pacemaker. I've already integrated APIs thinking that the supplier took care of everything, but this case shows that you can't trust blindly. One practice I recommend is to encrypt everything that passes through the API — use TLS 1.3 for data in transit and AES-256 for data stored locally. Another idea is to log each interaction, so you can see if someone is trying endless sessions to drain the battery or access where they shouldn't. It's the bare minimum to protect the data these devices send.

In the end, using third-party APIs in something as critical as a CIED requires more than just plug and play. The FDA in 2013 said there were no real attacks yet, but cases like the 2016 St. Jude recall of pacemakers after tests showed vulnerabilities, and the tweaks to Medtronic CareLink in 2018, tell me the risk is there. I've been through projects where I underestimated API security, but now I see that we need to be proactive: set up secure manual updates via USB, like Medtronic did, and monitor networks with tools like Wireshark to catch any strange traffic. This way, you ensure that patient data — and even their lives — do not end up in the hands of anyone who shouldn't get close.

PRIVACY IN ARTIFICIAL INTELLIGENCE AND MACHINE LEARNING APPLICATIONS

Privacy in artificial intelligence and machine learning applications has become a central topic as these models process large volumes of personal data. Machine learning algorithms often rely on large, detailed data sets to deliver accuracy, but this volume of information increases the risk of leaks and privacy violations. Protecting data at every stage of the AI lifecycle, from collection to inference, requires strategies that balance model performance with preserving user privacy.

One of the solutions that I have already mentioned here is the use of differential privacy, which ends up being widely used in machine learning models to protect data during training. This method adds mathematically calculated noise to the data or algorithm outputs so that the results remain useful for aggregate analysis but do not reveal information specific to an individual. Implementing differential privacy in a model requires defining parameters, such as noise level and privacy budget, that control the amount of protection offered without compromising the usefulness of the model.

Anonymization and pseudonymization techniques are widely used to prepare training datasets for AI. Anonymization removes information that could directly or indirectly identify an individual, while pseudonymization replaces identifiers with codes or tokens, maintaining the possibility of re-identification under controlled conditions. These practices significantly reduce the risks associated with breaches, but must be combined with other measures, such as encryption and access control, to provide broad protection.

The risks of data leakage in AI models are varied and can occur at different stages. Attacks such as membership inference can exploit trained models to determine whether a particular record was part of the training set. To mitigate these risks, limit access to training data, apply techniques such as differential privacy during model development, and perform regular testing to identify potential vulnerabilities in the algorithms or deployment environment.

Tools and frameworks designed to incorporate privacy into AI are indispensable allies in this context. Solutions like TensorFlow Privacy and PySyft help implement differential privacy and federated learning, while libraries like Meta's Opacus make it easy to integrate privacy measures into machine learning pipelines. These tools enable development teams to protect data without having to rewrite entire models, promoting a safer and more reliable AI environment.

In the context of AI, the AI Act, a regulation proposed by the European Union for artificial intelligence, has direct implications for privacy in AI and machine learning applications. Legislation classifies AI systems according to their level of risk, imposing requirements for those who deal with sensitive personal data. Models used for automated decisions, such as credit analysis and recruitment, will need to ensure transparency, explainability and bias mitigation. Furthermore, the AI Act reinforces the need to adopt privacy by design techniques, requiring AI systems to incorporate privacy safeguards by design, including regular audits and detailed records on data use. This approach seeks to balance innovation and protection of fundamental rights, creating a safer environment for the development and application of AI technologies.

The interplay between the AI Act and GDPR raises questions about potential legal ambiguities[60]. While both share principles such as transparency and accountability, they differ in scope and approach. The GDPR focuses on the protection of personal data, while the AI Act takes a broader perspective, also addressing aspects such as environmental protection and the rule of law. This overlap can result in legal uncertainty, especially when AI systems process personal data, requiring effective coordination between the two regulations.

One specific area of potential conflict is the processing of sensitive data. The GDPR generally prohibits the processing of this data except under specific circumstances. However, the AI Act introduces an exception that allows the use of sensitive data for monitoring and correcting biases in high-risk AI systems, provided that appropriate safeguards are implemented. This discrepancy can create challenges in the interpretation and application of laws, increasing the need for clear guidance to avoid legal uncertainties.

This is one of the greatest challenges facing the European Union, but the complexity is not limited to the bloc. Around the world, complementary AI regulations are requiring an integrated approach between legal and technical engineering to ensure compliance without stifling innovation. The balance between data protection, transparency and technological development helps create a regulatory environment that protects the rights of individuals without impeding the advancement of artificial intelligence.

BLOCKCHAIN: PRIVACY AND IMMUTABILITY

Blockchain, in essence, is a decentralized and immutable structure that records transactions in blocks interconnected by cryptography. Each block contains a set of transactions, a timestamp and a hash of the previous block, ensuring the integrity and continuity of the system. The technology gained notoriety with Bitcoin, but its uses extend beyond cryptocurrencies to include smart contracts, supply chain tracking and digital identities. Distributed design reduces the need for intermediaries while increasing transparency and resistance against malicious changes.

Imagine a group of multinational companies that need to exchange critical information daily, contract documents, production records, financial data. Each company has its own system, its own rules, and the exchange of this information has always generated conflicts. A common accusation was: "You changed the data!" or "That's not what we agreed upon!"

To solve this problem, a consortium of these companies decided to take a radically new approach: creating a distributed ledger. There would be no central server to control the information. Instead, everyone would have access to the same registry, but with a unique structure that would ensure it was immutable and transparent.

The system worked like this: each time a transaction took place, such as the delivery of a batch of electronic components, the information was transformed into a block of data. This block contained not only the details of the transaction, but also a kind of "fingerprint", a mathematically generated code called a hash. This hash wasn't just a unique mark of the current block; it was also connected to the hash of the previous block, forming a chain, a blockchain.

A fascinating feature of this system was that any attempt to alter an old block would immediately break the chain. For example, if someone tried to change the number of components delivered in a past transaction, the hash of the changed block would change, invalidating all subsequent blocks. And since each company had its own copy of the chain, any discrepancies would be immediately detected.

At first, some companies were suspicious. "How can we ensure that no one controls this system?" they asked. This is where decentralized architecture shined: consensus was the key. Whenever a new block was added, most companies needed to validate the transaction based on pre-established rules. If the majority agreed, the block was added to the chain. There was no centralized power, and decisions were based on mathematics and cryptography, not blind trust.

Over time, the system proved to be incredibly efficient. Smart contracts have been added to the blockchain, automating processes such as payments and deliveries. A contract could be programmed to automatically release payment when sensors confirmed delivery of components. It was fast, safe and transparent.

But the impact was not limited to operational efficiency. Companies realized that the system forced them to work more ethically. There was no way to tamper with production reports or hide delivery failures without everyone noticing. Blockchain didn't just record transactions; it created an environment where trust was guaranteed by technology.

This story is not a science fiction tale; It's a real transformation happening across sectors, from the financial industry to supply chains. Blockchain is not just a technology, but a new way of structuring trust in complex systems, where transparency and integrity are fundamental. Its true power is not in eliminating intermediaries, but in creating a model where no one needs to doubt the validity of the information, because the structure itself guarantees this. It is a system that does not require trust, because trust is built into the code.

The different types of blockchain can be mainly categorized as public and permissioned. Public blockchains such as Ethereum[61], are accessible to anyone, while permissioned ones, like Hyperledger Fabric[62], are designed for use in private consortia, where access control is strictly regulated. Each approach offers specific advantages and challenges, such as greater privacy in permissioned networks versus greater decentralization in public ones.

The relationship between blockchain and privacy laws is often contentious due to the intrinsic immutability of records. For example, the "right to be forgotten" is difficult to implement on blockchains, as data cannot simply be erased.

Alternatives to mitigate these challenges include side-chains, which function as auxiliary blockchains connected to the main one, allowing greater flexibility in privacy rules. Off-chain solutions store data outside the blockchain, leaving only cryptographic references or hashes in the ledger, thus protecting private information. Technologies like Hyperledger also offer modular frameworks that support anonymization and granular access control.

The European Parliamentary Research Service (EPRS) is an internal research service of the European Parliament, responsible for providing in-depth analysis and studies to support parliamentarians in their legislative and political decisions. Its mission is to ensure that European policymakers have access to impartial, detailed and evidence-based information, helping them understand complex issues and formulate more effective and well-informed policies.

Within this context, EPRS developed a guide[63] focused on the legal and technical challenges and implications of using emerging technologies, such as blockchain, in compliance with the General Data Protection Regulation (GDPR). The guide seeks to guide policymakers, companies and developers in navigating the regulatory and operational aspects of this technology, highlighting best practices for protecting personal data and ensuring privacy in decentralized networks.

The document provides a solid theoretical foundation and practical recommendations on how to implement blockchains in ways that respect fundamental data protection principles, including privacy by design and by default.

The guidance emphasizes that technologies like blockchain must incorporate privacy by design. This includes principles such as data minimization, use of pseudonymization, and ensuring that collection and processing are proportionately justifiable. The research body also encourages the use of impact assessments to identify risks and the implementation of preventive measures, in line with existing regulations, in addition to highlight that the use of blockchain requires adaptation to data protection laws, due to the intrinsic characteristics of the technology.

Blockchain must be designed to minimize privacy risks from the outset, adopting privacy by design and privacy by default principles. These practices include implementing measures such as pseudonymization, data minimization and carrying out data protection impact assessments (DPIAs). The guide reinforces that the focus must be on the proportionality between the collection and processing of data and the legitimate purposes that justify these actions.

A critical point addressed by EPRS is the role of the controller and operator in a blockchain environment. The controller is defined as the entity or person who determines the purposes and means of processing personal data. In permissioned blockchains, for example, the consortium members who establish the rules of the network are often considered the controllers. The operator, which can be a specific node or an entity that performs technical actions for the functioning of the blockchain, acts on behalf of the controller and, therefore, is bound by the terms established by the controller, as well as applicable legislation.

The issue of liability also comes to a halt where in permissioned networks, governance is generally centralized, and controllers are identifiable, which facilitates the attribution of legal responsibility. However, in public and decentralized blockchains, identifying a controller becomes complex, as there is no single entity or person determining the purposes of processing. In these cases, individual operators, such as miners or validators, may be held responsible for their specific contributions, depending on their ability to influence data processing.

Furthermore, the guide highlights that, in public blockchains, it is important to consider the adoption of auxiliary technologies to minimize the exposure of personal data. Solutions such as cryptographic hashes, pseudonymization and off-chain storage are recommended to reduce the volume of data stored directly on the blockchain. These approaches allow only irreversible data or references to be recorded in the ledger, protecting data subject rights and aligning with data protection requirements.

Finally, the EPRS points out that ultimate responsibility depends on the network architecture and participants' transparency about their roles. Permissioned networks have greater clarity around governance and accountability, while public blockchains require additional effort to define legal contracts and terms of use that meet local and international regulations. Thus, while blockchain technology has the potential to increase transparency and security, it also demands robust adaptation to ensure regulatory compliance and protect the rights of data subjects.

> As a practical example, in a supply chain system, use a side-chain to record only hashes of personal data (e.g.: SHA-256 from an email), keeping the details outside the main blockchain. This cuts the risk of direct exposure.

In conclusion, blockchain offers the potential to solve complex problems across diverse industries, but its application must be carefully architected to balance immutability and privacy. Hybrid solutions that combine permissioned blockchains with off-chain mechanisms show promise for meeting legal and operational requirements without compromising technological benefits.

ZERO-KNOWLEDGE PROOF (ZKP)

Zero-Knowledge Proof is a cryptographic technique that allows an individual (the prover) to demonstrate to another party (the verifier) that a statement is true without revealing any additional information beyond the veracity of the statement itself. In simple terms, the prover can convince the verifier that he possesses a certain knowledge or meets a specific condition without exposing underlying details. For example, ZKP can be used to prove that a person is of legal age without revealing their date of birth.

Once upon a time, in a medieval city, there was a merchant named Lucas who sold rare and expensive jewelry. Lucas had a secret: he knew where a safe full of precious diamonds was hidden, but he never wanted to reveal the location to anyone. One day, a nobleman appeared in his store, willing to buy a diamond, but wanted to ensure that Lucas actually had access to the safe before paying. The problem was that Lucas didn't trust the nobleman enough to show him the location of the hiding place. That's when Lucas had a brilliant idea.

He told the nobleman, "I will prove that I can access the safe without showing you where it is." Lucas then led the nobleman to a forest with many trails, all leading to an identical entry point. Lucas entered one of the trails alone and, after a few minutes, he appeared again with a diamond in his hands. The nobleman was impressed, as Lucas clearly demonstrated that he had access to the safe, but without revealing which trail was the right one or where the diamonds were hidden.

Just as Lucas was able to prove that he knew something (the location of the safe) without revealing the secret itself, ZKP allows someone to demonstrate the veracity of information without sharing the underlying data. This technique is used in modern systems to protect privacy, such as in financial transactions, where it is possible to check whether someone has enough balance for a purchase without exposing their bank statement or personal details.

The importance of ZKP for privacy and data protection lies in its ability to minimize information exposure during checks or transactions. In scenarios where people data is involved, such as authentication, financial transactions or identity checks, ZKP can eliminate the need to share information beyond what is necessary. This meets the principle of data minimization and significantly reduces the risk of leaks and breaches since the underlying data is not transmitted or stored.

Software engineers can use ZKP in various projects to increase privacy and security. In authentication systems, for example, ZKP can be employed to validate login credentials without transferring passwords or sensitive identifiers. In blockchains, this technique is used to carry out private transactions, allowing valueoors and participants remain anonymous while the integrity of the transaction is verified. In identity verification systems, ZKP can ensure that a person meets certain criteria (such as being a resident of a specific country) without exposing other personal data.

The case of the World Network[64] involving the collection of biometric data from the human iris against payment to issue a digital identity has sparked broad debates about privacy and security. The World Network uses devices called Orb, which capture images of users' irises to generate a unique identification, known as World ID. This data is used to create a digital identity linked to a decentralized system. In exchange for participation, the Users receive financial rewards such as the Worldcoin (WLD) token. The goal is to create a global proof-of-humanity infrastructure that can be used for different purposes, such as preventing bots, authenticating transactions and enabling universal access to the digital economy.

One of the central technical aspects of the project is the use of Zero-Knowledge Proofs (ZKP), an advanced cryptographic technique that allows users to prove that they have a valid World ID without revealing additional information about their identityage or biometrics. This ensures that captured biometric data is processed and stored locally on the Orb device and is never transmitted in its entirety to central servers. Only identification codes are used for verification, which significantly reduces the risks of exposing sensitive personal data.

The decision to use ZKP is especially important because it balances the demands for privacy with the need for reliable authentication on a global scale. This mechanism prevents third parties, including World Network itself, from having direct access to users' iris images or other personal information. World Network seeks to ensure that each individual's identity is unique and non-transferable, even in the event of attempted fraud or compromised credentials.

Despite these advanced security measures, collecting biometric data for a fee has raised ethical and regulatory concerns. Critics argue that offering financial incentives could lead vulnerable populations to share their data without fully understanding the risks. The reliability of device-based systems like Orb is also questioned, especially in relation to the possibility of physical or technical attacks that compromise the security of the devices.

The implementation of ZKP requires familiarity with specialized libraries and frameworks. Tools like zk-SNARKs and zk-

STARKs offer robust frameworks for integrating ZKP into modern systems. Additionally, languages like Rust, which have dedicated libraries for ZKP, can be useful. It is important that engineers understand not only the mathematical foundations of ZKP, but also its practical application, ensuring that the technology is used efficiently and safely.

For example, in an anonymous voting system, use zk-SNARKs to ensure that the vote is valid without showing who voted. With snarkjs, create a circuit that checks if the age is greater than 18, generates the proof with groth16.full and then proves and validates with groth16.verify. Start with something small to get the hang of it, like basics with the library *snarkjs* em Javascript:

```javascript
const { groth16 } = require("snarkjs");
// Proof generation and verification (simplified)

const proof = await groth16.fullProve({ input: 18 },
"circuit.wasm", "zkey");

const verified = await groth16.verify("verification_key.json",
proof);

console.log("Valid vote?", verified);
```

This proves that the user is over 18 without exposing their exact age. Of course, the example above is quite simplified, just to demonstrate what a practical implementation of the beating heart of a ZKP test would look like, however, the entire system and infrastructure that conditions this execution needs to be designed and designed to fulfill the same purpose.

Finally, the adoption of ZKP is a significant step towards meeting the increasingly demanding privacy standards in the market. Its application can transform systems into more reliable solutions, protecting both user data and the reputation of organizations. Software engineers who master this technology can not only solve technical challenges, but also add strategic value to projects that seek to differentiate themselves through their commitment to privacy and security.

SOFTWARE TESTING FOR PRIVACY

Testing tools are essential components for ensuring security and privacy in systems. In the security context, solutions such as OWASP ZAP (Zed Attack Proxy) and Burp Suite are widely used to identify vulnerabilities in web applications. These tools allow you to simulate attacks such as SQL injections and exploit XSS flaws, providing detailed insights into weaknesses in the system. For privacy testing, tools like Databunker help audit the use of personal data, evaluating whether data collection, storage and sharing practices are aligned with established standards. Additionally, automation frameworks like Selenium can be integrated to validate data flows involving personal information.

The role of the DPO (Data Protection Officer) in requesting security and privacy test reports is critical to keeping the organization compliant. The DPO may require the IT team to present documented evidence of testing performed, such as vulnerability scan logs, attack simulation results, and privacy compliance audits. These reports should include details such as identified vulnerabilities, associated risks, and implemented corrective actions. Additionally, the DPO can charge specific metrics, such as the percentage of issues resolved versus discovered, and ensure that testing is performed periodically.

Ensuring proven security in systems is a constant challenge for IT teams, mainly due to the increasing complexity of architectures and the volume of data processed. Running regular tests requires time, resources, and expertise, which can be a hindrance in environments with tight deadlines. Additionally, IT faces the challenge of maintaining traceable records of tests performed, ensuring that all evidence is available for future audits. Implementing secure CI/CD pipelines with automated validation steps and integration of security tools helps mitigate these challenges and increase process efficiency.

OWASP, a global reference in application security, provides a solid foundation for structuring tests, with projects such as the OWASP Top Ten, which lists the main vulnerabilities in web systems, and the OWASP Security Knowledge Framework, which guides teams on how to build secure applications. Using these guidelines in conjunction with specific tools ensures that testing practices are sufficient and effective, covering everything from detecting technical failures to analyzing compliance with privacy principles such as data minimization and access control.

Finally, alignment between the DPO and the IT team is necessary for successful security and privacy testing. While the DPO defines the goals and regulatory requirements to be met, IT implements the tools and performs technical checks. This collaboration guarantees not only the security of the systems, but also the creation of an environment of trust, where data protection is treated as a strategic priority. Tools such as JIRA or Trello can be used to centralize the management of tickets related to tests and audits, ensuring traceability and efficient communication between teams.

CHECKLIST OF PRACTICAL ACTIONS

☐ Configured security scans in the CI/CD pipeline (e.g.: Snyk on GitHub Actions) since the beginning of the project.
☐ Modeled threats to identify risks at each stage of the project.
☐ Validated inputs and outputs to prevent injections and

---

script attacks.

☐ Applied strong authentication and access control in all applications.

☐ Integrated security and compliance into CI/CD pipelines.

☐ Continuously monitored vulnerabilities in libraries and external dependencies.

☐ Configured tools for static and dynamic code analysis.

☐ Performed penetration tests on third-party APIs with OWASP ZAP and validated compliance with privacy policies.

☐ Performed regular tests to check the impact of code changes.

☐ Documented all vulnerabilities identified and corrective actions taken.

☐ Used frameworks like OWASP ZAP to test applications against the main threats.

☐ Validated that data manipulated by APIs is protected against unauthorized access

FINAL
CONSIDERATIONS

When I dove headfirst into the privacy market, I wanted to write something useful that would show technicians how to put these concepts into practice without complications.

During my own learning journey, I realized that there was space for this type of content as most of the available materials focused on legal and regulatory aspects, often leaving aside the question I heard most from technical professionals: "How to implement this in practice?".

This work was my attempt to fill this void and offer a guide that connects theory to practice, albeit in a very summarized way so that you can seek more data and resources for your own implementation.

Still, it's important to remember that the technical aspects are just one piece of the puzzle. Implementing a privacy program requires a solid understanding of the legal, ethical and organizational foundations. These knowledge domains form the foundation upon which technical solutions are built. Knowing how to interpret regulations and understand the rights of data subjects, for example, is essential to align technical practices with broader privacy and data protection objectives.

For the next steps in your journey, I suggest you evaluate what stage you are at. If you are already familiar with the fundamentals of privacy and applicable regulations, delving deeper into privacy governance programs could be an excellent next step. This includes exploring how to integrate privacy into organizational processes, measuring the maturity of data protection practices, and implementing methodologies that ensure ongoing compliance in dynamic corporate environments.

To advance, try hands-on projects like setting up a secure server with Nginx and LetsEncrypt, or explore certifications like CIPT (IAPP), Exin, or ISACA. Tools like Wireshark (traffic analysis) and OpenSSL (encryption) are great starting points. Sign up to communities like OWASP Brasil to exchange experiences.

If this book has been your introduction to the world of privacy and data protection, I recommend that you begin to consolidate your understanding of the fundamental concepts. Terms like informational self-determination, data minimization, and privacy by design are not just words; they represent principles that guide all technical and company decisions in a privacy program. Investing time in understanding these concepts is the first step to building a solid foundation.

Regardless of where you are on your journey, be sure to seek constant updating. The field of privacy is evolving rapidly, driven by technological advances and new regulations. Keeping up with trends such as responsible artificial intelligence, neurotechnology, security in IoT devices and privacy in cloud environments will allow you to always be prepared for market challenges. Participating in communities, events and discussion groups is also a valuable way to share experiences and learn from other professionals.

Additionally, maintain a practical and collaborative mindset. Privacy and data protection are not problems that can be solved in isolation. They require collaboration between areas such as information security, software development, legal and compliance. Being a facilitator in this interdisciplinary dialogue is an essential skill for any professional in the field.

Ultimately, I hope this book has provided valuable insights and inspiration for you to continue exploring this fascinating field. More than just implementing technical solutions, working with privacy is an opportunity to contribute to a more ethical and respectful world towards people and their data. I hope this book helps you take a step forward.I've learned the hard way trying to force privacy into rushed projects — but I've seen it's worth it. Good luck, and anything, we'll see you out there in the tech communities!

GLOSSARY

Although the book is aimed at a more technical audience, I understand that some terms are not familiar to every professional's day-to-day life, so I prepared this glossary with simple explanations about each term. To better understand some concepts, you will need to seek more detailed training.

Term	Explanation
Added-noise measurement obfuscation	Technique that adds statistical noise to data to protect privacy without changing overall trends. Used in differential privacy.
Anonymity Set	Set of individuals in a dataset where each one is indistinguishable from at least k-1 others, making identification difficult (based on k-anonymity).
Attribute Based Credentials	Authentication method that reveals only specific attributes (e.g. 'over 18') without exposing complete data such as name or date of birth.
DevSecOps	Approach that integrates security into the development and operations cycle,

	automating controls from conception to deployment.
Do Not Track (DNT)	HTTP header that allows the user to indicate a preference for not being tracked online, although it depends on voluntary opt-in from websites.
DPIA (Data Protection Impact Assessment)	Data protection impact assessment to identify and mitigate risks in projects that process personal information.
Hardening	Process of strengthening systems security by removing vulnerabilities such as unnecessary services or excessive permissions.
Hyperledger	Permissioned blockchain framework for private networks, focusing on access control and privacy in business consortia.
Identity Federation	Authentication system that allows single sign-on (SSO) between services, without the identity provider tracking all access.
K-anonymous	Anonymization technique that guarantees that each record in a dataset is indistinguishable from at least k-1 others,

	reducing re-identification risks.
Location Granularity	Minimization principle that adjusts the accuracy of the collected location (e.g., city rather than exact coordinates) to protect privacy.
Masquerade	Technique where the user provides altered or filtered data (e.g. alternative email) to hide their real identity.
Onion Routing	Routing method that encrypts data in layers and passes it through multiple nodes (e.g. Tor), hiding origin and destination.
P3P (Platform for Privacy Preferences)	W3C standard that facilitates the communication of privacy policies between websites and browsers, currently little used.
Privacy by Default	Principle that configures systems to protect privacy by default, without requiring user action (e.g. cookies disabled by default).
Privacy by Design	Approach that incorporates privacy from the design of systems, considering it at all stages of development.
Privacy Differential	Technique that adds controlled noise to data or algorithm

	results to protect individual information without compromising aggregate analysis.
Pseudonymous Identity	Use of alternative identifiers (e.g. pseudonyms) that do not reveal the real identity, but allow consistent interactions.
Pseudonymous Messaging	Communication via pseudonyms or intermediaries, hiding the real sender and recipient (e.g.: disposable emails).
RBAC (Role-Based Access Control)	Role-based access control, where permissions are assigned according to the user's role in the system.
Side-chains	Auxiliary blockchains connected to the main one, allowing flexibility in privacy rules without changing the original ledger.
Strip Invisible Metadata	Technique that removes hidden metadata (e.g. EXIF in photos) to avoid exposing personal data such as location.
TC String	String used in the IAB TCF to store and transmit user consent preferences in digital advertising.

Tokenization	Replacement of sensitive data with unique tokens, keeping the originals in a secure vault, used to protect information in tests or transactions.
Zero-Knowledge Proof (ZKP)	Cryptographic technique that proves the veracity of a statement (e.g. 'I am of legal age') without revealing additional information beyond that.
zk-SNARKs	Type of ZKP (Zero-Knowledge Succinct Non-Interactive Argument of Knowledge) used in blockchains for private and efficient verifications.

[1]   https://www.cloudflare.com/pt-br/learning/security/glossary/what-is-zero-trust/

[2] https://aws.amazon.com/what-is/api/

[3] https://security.virginia.edu/deepfakes

[4] https://www.fortunebusinessinsights.com/data-privacy-software-market-105420

[5]   https://www.grandviewresearch.com/industry-analysis/privacy-management-software-market-report

[6] https://online.utulsa.edu/blog/data-privacy-officer/

[7] Warren, Samuel D., and Louis D. Brandeis. "The Right to Privacy." *Harvard Law Review*, vol. 4, no. 5, 1890, pp. 193–220. *JSTOR*, https://doi.org/10.2307/1321160. Accessed 9 Feb. 2025.

[8] Sarlet, Ingo Wolfgang. "Protection of personal data as a fundamental right in the Brazilian federal constitution of 1988." *Fundamental Rights & Justice* (2020).

[9]   https://techcrunch.com/2025/02/06/openai-launches-data-residency-in-europe/

[10]   https://www.edps.europa.eu/data-protection/our-work/subjects/eprivacy-directive_en

[11]   https://www.government.nl/topics/european-union/question-and-answer/what-is-brexit

[12] https://iapp.org/resources/global-privacy-directory/

[13]   https://www.europarl.europa.eu/RegData/etudes/ATAG/2020/652073/EPRS_ATA(2020)652073_EN.pdf

[14] A. Cavoukian, "PbD origin and evolution," Privacy by Design, 2012; http://privacybydesign.ca/

[15] https://www.ibm.com/think/topics/devsecops

[16] https://privacypatterns.org/

[17] https://iapp.org/resources/article/privacy-program-management/

[18] https://en.wikipedia.org/wiki/Ann_Cavoukian

[19] https://www.ibm.com/think/topics/end-to-end-encryption

[20] Cavoukian, Ann. "Privacy by design [leading edge]." IEEE Technology and Society Magazine 31.4 (2012): 18-19.

[21] https://gs.statcounter.com/

[22]Classen, J., Chen, Y.-S., Steinmetzer, D., Hollick, M., & Knightly, E. (2021). *Attacks on Wireless Coexistence: Exploiting Cross-Technology Performance Features for Inter-Chip Privilege Escalation.* arXiv preprint arXiv:2112.05719. Available at: https://arxiv.org/pdf/2112.05719. Accessed on: March 2, 2025

[23] https://www.geeksforgeeks.org/repository-design-pattern/

[24] https://en.wikipedia.org/wiki/Data_access_layer

[25] https://en.wikipedia.org/wiki/Transparent_data_encryption

[26] https://proxysql.com/

[27] https://www.pgbouncer.org/

[28] https://aws.amazon.com/pt/kms/

[29] https://azure.microsoft.com/pt-br/products/key-vault

[30] https://aws.amazon.com/pt/rds/

[31] https://www.keycloak.org/

[32] https://jwt.io/

[33] https://www.gpdp.it/web/guest/home/docweb/-/docweb-display/docweb/9988921

[34] https://www.terraform.io/

[35] https://docs.ansible.com/

[36] https://www.splunk.com/

[37] https://www.elastic.co/pt/elastic-stack

[38] https://github.com/tensorflow/privacy

[39] https://github.com/google/differential-privacy

[40] https://github.com/tensorflow/privacy

[41] https://arxiv.org/abs/cs/0610105

[42] https://petsymposium.org/popets/2023/popets-2023-0043.php

[43] https://linddun.org/ - Linddun methodology website

[44] Article 29 Working Party (2018) Guidelines on Consent under Regulation 2016/679 (last revised and adopted on 10 April 2018), 17/EN, WP259 rev.01. https://ec.europa.eu/newsroom/article29/item-detail.cfm?item_id=623051

[45] https://digiday.com/sponsored/why-publishers-are-ready-to-end-the-high-cost-of-third-party-cookies-and-data-leakage/

[46] Doneda, Danilo. "The protection of personal data as a fundamental right." *Legal Space: Journal of Law* 12.2 (2011): 91-108.

[47] https://edition.cnn.com/2024/02/04/asia/deepfake-cfo-scam-hong-kong-intl-hnk/index.html

[48] https://www.bbc.com/news/technology-49252501

[49] https://www.washingtonpost.com/technology/2022/05/31/abolish-privacy-policies/

[50] https://twitterdatadash.com/

[51] https://en.wikipedia.org/wiki/STRIDE_model

[52] https://threat-modeling.com/pasta-threat-modeling/

[53] https://techcrunch.com/2019/05/01/ladders-resume-leak/?guccounter=1

[54] http://securityweek.com/millions-of-user-records-stolen-from-65-websites-via-sql-injection-attacks/

[55] https://sqlmap.org/

[56] https://cve.mitre.org/

[57] https://nvd.nist.gov/

[58] https://www.theguardian.com/technology/2022/nov/28/meta-fined-265m-over-data-breach-affecting-more-than-500m-users

[59] Kapoor A, Vora A, Yadav R. Cardiac devices and cyber attacks: How far are they real? How to overcome? Indian Heart J. 2019 Nov-Dec;71(6):427-430. doi: 10.1016/j.ihj.2020.02.001. PMID: 32248912; PMCID: PMC7136318.

[60] https://ansabrasil.com.br/english/news/science_tecnology/2025/02/28/interaction-between-ai-act-and-gdpr-risks-legal-uncertainty_ef33e5e8-7880-4872-be65-424c54c9c83f.html

[61] https://ethereum.org/

[62] https://www.ibm.com/br-pt/topics/hyperledger

[63]   https://www.europarl.europa.eu/RegData/etudes/
STUD/2019/634445/EPRS_STU(2019)634445_EN.pdf

[64] https://whitepaper.world.org/

ABOUT THE AUTHOR

Marison Souza

Co-founder of Privacy Tools, the largest Brazilian platform for privacy and data protection. Software engineer, judicial expert, and privacy specialist with certifications from Harvard University and ECPC from Maastricht University.